BLANK CANVAS

BLANK CANVAS

HOW I REINVENTED
MY LIFE AFTER PRISON

CRAIG STANLAND

LIONCREST
PUBLISHING

BLANK CANVAS

How I Reinvented My Life after Prison

ISBN   978-1-5445-1948-7   *Hardcover*

   978-1-5445-1947-0   *Paperback*

   978-1-5445-1946-3   *Ebook*

FOR MY FAMILY AND FRIENDS

ONE

"The price of anything is the amount of life you exchange for it."
–HENRY DAVID THOREAU

OCTOBER 1, 2013

You have one unheard voicemail.

"Mr. Stanland, this is Special Agent McTiernan with the FBI. We are at your residence and have a warrant for your arrest. You will need to call us and come home immediately, or we will issue an APB with the federal marshals for your arrest."

My lungs can't find air. It's quiet, except for my heart. It's pumping so hard it's on the verge of giving up or bursting out of my chest. My mind is trying to comprehend what I just heard. I don't know what the fuck to do. I know I want to rip off my skin and leave this place. A voice whispered to me; it was always there, but I always ignored it. The FBI sitting in my house made it impossible to ignore it anymore.

The voice says only one thing: *I told you so.*

I stare at my desk and what was supposed to be the beginning of my workday. An unopened laptop sits on my desk with its power cord sitting on top of it, still neatly wrapped, my black spiral notebook and pen to the right.

I glance over the top of my cube and take inventory of the office. It's Tuesday morning, not quite nine o'clock, people are just starting to trickle in. Someone just put on the morning pot of coffee.

I can't remember anyone's name; I only started this job two weeks ago. I'm surrounded by strangers. I don't know what to do.

What will they think? *Why is the new guy about to walk out of the office he just walked into?* How do I make that make sense? Excuses race through my brain—a family emergency, sudden illness, a client meeting—anything to get me out of here unnoticed. But that seems impossible. I feel like the voicemail was broadcast for everyone to hear. A neon sign flashes "FBI Most Wanted" above my head. Time stands still and everyone knows.

I snap out of it. The thought of the marshals busting in at any moment scares me into action. I gather my belongings and walk through the office. I try to sneak out as the neon sign follows my every move. I feel more conspicuous the more inconspicuous I try to be.

The thirty-six-floor elevator ride to the lobby takes forever. I keep my head down as I pass the security desk and walk out of the building. Rush hour in New York City: the sidewalk is a sea of people; cab drivers lean on their horns; sirens wail in the distance; my heart races past it all. The noise is unbearable. I'm surrounded by thousands of people and utterly alone.

Handing the parking attendant my slip, I feel the need to apologize for parking for only twenty minutes when I told him it would be nine hours. "I forgot I had a meeting..."

He doesn't seem to care either way, although I swear he knows the truth.

Usually, I enjoy driving the West Side Highway, taking in the views: the Hudson River, the city skyline, the George Washington Bridge, people exercising in Riverside Park, kids playing soccer. I'm envious of the runners, enjoying their freedom. It's a beautiful drive on most days. Not now. None of it registers. It's all a blur, like my thoughts.

What's happening? Is Kyla okay? What am I driving into? What's waiting for me?

This is a mistake, a misunderstanding. When I get home, we'll sit down and sort this out, I think with hollow optimism, my brain entering survival mode. Deep down, I know this is the end. It's caught up with me.

I call home, falling further and further away from her with each unanswered ring. I imagine her big, beautiful smile from this morning, her golden hair still messy from a good night's sleep. Just this morning, I kissed her goodbye.

She answers after seven excruciating rings. "Craig, what's happening?"

She speaks through trembling lips. The confidence and strength are gone from her voice, replaced with fear, confusion, and betrayal. I feel myself shrinking as her emotions rip through me.

I imagine her petite frame sitting on the edge of our bed, one hand holding the phone, the other holding her head as she fights to keep it together.

She's living the fear I'm only thinking about. Surrounded by FBI agents, she's afraid to speak. I can't answer her question. I don't know what to say. All I can think of is, "Call my father."

Why is this happening now?

Only a few weeks earlier, we had one of those conversations couples need to have when life spins out of control. We discussed how we're both unhappy and that our lives need to change. How the life we were living was not the life that we'd envisioned for our relationship. We were open and honest. We listened to each other without judgment.

We were spending way too much money on things that didn't matter, expensive dinners and bottles of wine. Each of us watching our alcohol consumption escalate, each of us trying to escape this life we created. We were intertwined and dependent on the presence of each other, moving further away from who we are and who we wanted to be. Two beautiful, strong people lost in the wake of each other.

We talked about how much better life would be if we put that money aside, created some security. What if we rebuilt our lives, not chasing each day, but building a future together? What if we pursued experiences, not things? With that conversation, my new job, and her new business, we started a new chapter of our lives. This was an opportunity to return to who we were and whom we had fallen in love with. This was our second chance.

I had stopped the fraud—there was no need to lie anymore and it was pure relief. I didn't understand the burden I was carrying until it was gone. Life felt right. It felt good.

* * *

With each passing mile, I feel like I'm driving into the end of our relationship, our second chance destroyed before we even had the opportunity to try. I keep thinking, *I'm going to lose her.*

I drive through the gates of our community, wanting to go back to that moment but knowing I couldn't be any further from it.

As I turn down the hill, the scene comes into view: Law enforcement vehicles are parked everywhere; dozens of agents stand in the street. One of them identifies my car, points, and says something I cannot hear. They all turn around. Slowly, I pull into a parking spot. The agents approach me cautiously, hands on their weapons, ready for whatever may happen. I don't know why I'm surprised that they really do wear blue jackets with "FBI" written in yellow like on TV.

I can barely open the car door; the agents are controlling me with their bodies. Slowly I stand up, my back pressed against the car. An agent approaches me, gray suit, square jaw, tight haircut, and he stands inches away from my face. I'm intimidated by him.

"Identify yourself and slowly empty the contents of your pockets onto the front seat."

"Craig Stanland."

He nods.

I place my keys, cellphone, a USB drive, and a pen on the front seat. The agents systematically take inventory of each item, carefully putting everything into Ziploc sandwich bags. I regret not hiding my cellphone. They turn me around, frisk me, and then turn me back.

I think of her, wishing I could hold her. To let her know it's going to be alright. I'd be lying, but I want to protect her. I thought of our conversation, wishing I could go back to that moment.

"Can I see my wife? Can I go inside? Please let me see her."

Under no circumstance would they allow us to see each other. They need to ensure there is no co-conspiracy. They wouldn't even allow eye contact from across the courtyard that stands between us.

An FBI agent reads me my rights as he pulls handcuffs from his waistband.

"You don't need to cuff me. I'm not a threat. Please don't cuff me."

I'm still holding onto the hope that this is a misunderstanding. I know the finality of handcuffs means it isn't.

"It's procedure," he says. "There's no way around it."

I put my hands behind my back, the cold metal snaps around my wrists. They're heavier than I thought they would be. I look around. Some of my neighbors are watching the scene unfold behind the safety of their curtains. Our neighbor Carl ducks out of view when our eyes meet. The agent places his hand on the back of my head, guiding me into a black unmarked car.

One agent sits in the driver's seat, another next to me in the back seat. The agent in the back seat begins questioning me. "We found multiple toothbrushes in your guest bathroom. Who else is involved?"

We kept spare toothbrushes for friends and family. It never crossed my mind that this could indicate a conspiracy.

"It was just me. No one else."

He looks at me incredulously and digs a little deeper. "How about that pretty, little fucking wife of yours?"

Whatever button he was trying to push, he found it. I'm fucking pissed and I'm helpless to do anything about it. The handcuffs have erased any courage that may have remained. I'm defenseless.

"She had nothing to do with it."

The agent's phone rings. "Yeah. Yeah, he's right here. Hold on."

The agent holds the phone to my ear. I have no idea who could be calling me.

"Mr. Stanland, this is Agent Johnson. I'm in your home and trying to access your laptop, the Dell. We need the password."

I use that laptop every single day and I have no clue. I start rattling off every password I can think of. None of them works.

The agent on the phone is getting frustrated. I apologize, "I'm sorry; I'm sorry. I don't know what it is."

"Fine. I can get into it. I was just hoping to avoid that route. Let me speak to Agent McTiernan."

They exchange a few words and the call ends.

I need to get out of this; I need out of these cuffs; I need to get away from this guy. I flashback to high school, thinking about what my friends and I did when we got parking tickets. We would search for any mistakes that would get the ticket thrown out in court. Was the license plate correct? The make and model of the car? The color? Anything, so we didn't have to pay the five dollars.

"Can I see the arrest and search warrants?"

"Everything is in order. You don't need to see them. Why do you need to, what do you expect to find? You won't understand it anyway."

"I'd like to see it."

Please let there be something to make this go away.

Not hiding his annoyance, he holds the warrant in front of me. "Fine, here, have fun. Tell me when to turn the page."

The thickness of the documents makes me understand the amount of work that took place to do all of this. I don't see any typos and he's right. I'm not sure what I am looking at. The moment I tell him that I'm done, he goes back to the questions.

"Where were you on September 11, 2013?"

One of my clients was devastated by the attacks on the World Trade Center. They hold a charity event every year in memory of that tragic day. I've attended every year. "I was at a charity event with my client."

"Don't fucking lie to me. That's not how you want to do this."

I didn't think I was lying. I thought that was where I was. The tone of his voice tells me that it's not where I was and that it's time to invoke my right to silence. He makes me second-guess myself, telling me how this is a terrible mistake.

"You sure you want to do that? I can still help you, but if you invoke, there is nothing I can do for you down the road. You'll be on your own. You sure?"

I think about it for a moment and second-guess myself as I say, "Yes."

"One last question. You don't have to answer, 'Why did you do it?'"

For some reason, I felt the need to answer honestly. "I needed the money."

He nods, tells the agent in the front, "Let's go." The agent starts the car, puts it in gear, and we drive away.

My wife, my home, my life: shrinking in the rearview mirror.

TWO

*"This I ever held worse that all certitude, to
know not what the worst ahead might be."*
—ALGERNON CHARLES SWINBURNE

I STARE AT THE FAMILIAR LANDSCAPE AS WE DRIVE NORTH
on Route 95. The agent behind the wheel is texting and making
calls as he weaves in and out of late-morning traffic. He's speaking to someone who is wherever we are going, preparing them
for our arrival. I don't know where we're going or what happens
next.

Nobody is telling me anything and I'm afraid to ask.

The agent in the back seat is creeping me out. I can't put my
finger on it. There's an aura surrounding him, like walking into
a house and getting the chills. Since I invoked, he can't speak
about the case. Instead, he's talking about the best pizza places
in Connecticut and how hot the women in Greenwich are. I
can't push myself any further away from him; my elbow is digging into the car door.

Both of their faces light up when one of them tells me that, due to the government shutdown, "Everyone there today volunteered to arrest you for no pay."

Lucky me.

We arrive at our destination, the federal courthouse in Bridgeport, an ominous building behind a security gate and chain-link fence. The loading dock doors open and we pull into an underground garage. The driver opens my door and I stand to the side of the car as the agents secure their weapons in the trunk.

* * *

Security buzzes us into the building. It's quiet. The only sound is the hum of the lights and our feet on the floor.

We take a short elevator ride and arrive at a room with three men. I see two federal marshals and another criminal in a beige jumpsuit. The other criminal is escorted out of the room as we walk in. I wonder, *Will I have to wear a beige jumpsuit?*

I'm confused by one of the marshals. He looks like a biker—long, red beard, a sleeve of tattoos, eyes as cold as steel. The other fits the federal marshal mold in my mind: former military, Izod shirt tucked into pressed khakis, tall and athletic, high and tight haircut.

I wouldn't mess with either of them regardless of the situation.

The former military marshal places me on a stool in the corner of the room, the height chart for mugshot photos behind me. I'm relieved that he's the one I'll be interacting with. The biker frightens me. I watch as the FBI agents discuss who will take credit for my arrest. I'm the prize at the bottom of a Cracker Jack box.

"Who should we put down as the arresting officer?"

The agent from the back seat is playing it cool. "Whatever… doesn't matter to me."

"Yeah, it doesn't matter to me eith…"

The creepy agent pounces on the opportunity. "I'll take it!"

It turns out it was a good move for him. Several months later, he received a citation, his investigation of my case being a significant factor. He doesn't hide his smile as he completes the paperwork.

These handcuffs are killing me. An old rotator cuff injury is coming back to life. I'm squirming as quietly as possible to get comfortable when it happens—my right hand slips out of the cuffs. Instantly my shoulder feels better and I panic. No one noticed, their heads are buried in paperwork, the creepy agent is still smiling. I must alert them. I don't want them thinking I'm planning an escape.

I slowly raise my hands in the air to reinforce that I have no weapon, that I am no threat. "Umm…"

Everyone's head snaps up simultaneously, stopping in their tracks, the room is dead silent, it's as though no one is breathing.

"My shoulder was bothering me and this happened," I say, moving my eyes to the cuffs dangling from my left wrist.

All eyes are on me. The biker looks like he wants to kill me. I don't dare breathe or move. My heart is freaking out. I'm going to be attacked or shot for trying to escape. The marshals slowly turn their gaze to the FBI agents, incredulous rage in their eyes.

"Jesus Christ, thank God he's not dangerous."

I can breathe again. The marshals and agents agree I'm not a threat and remove the cuffs—a small moment of comfort in an uncomfortable situation.

The military marshal walks toward me with military precision, stopping inches away from my face. "We are going to process you now."

I'm already in place for the mugshots. All I have to do is stand, face the camera, then turn to the right and then to the left. Fingerprinting and DNA collection followed: cotton swabs swirled around the inside of my mouth. The military marshal orders me to strip naked. I slowly remove my clothes, down to my boxers, thinking this was what he meant. He looks at me, frustration in his eyes.

"Everything."

I take them off and cover myself, feeling embarrassed as I try to keep up with his set of commands.

"Run your fingers through your hair; pull out your bottom gum; open your mouth wide as possible; arms above your head, then out to the sides; rotate your palms up and down; right foot up; left foot up; lift your testicles, turn around, spread your ass cheeks, squat, and cough."

The last command confuses me. I can't grasp what the hell he is saying. I've never heard those words in that sequence before. "I'm sorry, what?"

With a little more volume, he barks, "Turn around, spread your ass cheeks, squat, and cough."

It's as though he's speaking a foreign language. "I'm sorry, I'm not understanding."

This time there is no confusion; his eyes cut through mine as he screams, "TURN AROUND. SPREAD YOUR ASS CHEEKS. SQUAT AND COUGH."

I do as I'm told.

I stand, naked and humiliated, as he inspects my clothes. He wrings each piece of clothing like he's searching for water. Inch by inch, it's hypnotic how methodical he is. He looks me up and down and declares, "Mr. Stanland, you are now the property of the federal marshal."

He hands my clothes back to me and I get dressed as quickly as possible. Somehow, through all of this, I'm annoyed he wrinkled my John Varvatos pants.

The marshal places his arm through mine and walks me to a steel door. I don't know what's happening.

"I'm sorry, but where are we going? What happens next?"

Looking at me as though I'm an idiot, he replies, "Your arraignment."

After a long series of hallways and an elevator ride, we reach a wooden door, very different than every other door we walked through. The marshal lifts his right leg up to the magnetic reader. The door clicks open. Apparently, he keeps his security card in the cargo pocket. We walk into a courtroom. He places me in the juror's box. The only times I've ever been in court were for the occasional speeding ticket, never on this side.

I have a clear view of the entire courtroom. I look around, taking it all in. People are milling about. Some of them stop and stare at me.

A door opens. I turn to look. A bailiff is escorting Kyla to her seat. We haven't seen each other for hours. Even under these circumstances, she looks beautiful in slacks and a white top, her hair pulled neatly into a bun.

Her skin is pale and the burden of the day weighs on her shoulders. Her eye color changes with her emotions and they were a brilliant green the day we were married. Now they're the color of a storm cloud before it releases its first drop.

I feel her pain from across the room; I want to rush over and hold her, to tell her it will be all right. I also want to hide. I'm scared to face her. She turns toward me; our eyes meet. We smile at one another. It's the kind of smile people share when life isn't okay but we're trying to convince the other person it is. And maybe ourselves.

Our smiles are interrupted by the bailiff. "Please rise, the Honorable Judge Garfield presiding."

The judge takes his seat behind the bench. In his mid-sixties, he's got a gentle face, gray beard, and glasses. Holding a manila folder, he places it in front of him. He pushes the robe's sleeves to his elbow as he reviews the documents and begins to speak.

When a Formula One car is pushed beyond its limits, it shuts down. A safety feature to protect the engine. My mind reached its limit; it's shut down. I don't know what he's saying or what's going on. Suddenly, with crystal-clear clarity, my ears tune in.

"...the count of mail fraud carries a maximum sentence of twenty years in prison and a $250,000 fine."

A cry escapes Kyla's mouth as her head falls into her hands. It's the most primal sound I've ever heard. It's the sound of something breaking.

Twenty years. My life is over.

The proceedings come to an end. I make bail thanks to my father and Kyla, the cosigners of the $100,000 agreement.

The agents watch as I approach her, uncertainty hovering as I get closer. I wish the agents would give us this moment.

Timidly, I ask, "Are you okay?"

"Yes," she says. She's trying to be strong—either for me or for herself, I don't know—but her voice betrays her.

Both of us know there is nothing okay about any of this.

I want to reach for her hand, to feel her skin on mine but I'm afraid of her reaction.

As we walk out of the courthouse, I'm grateful for not leaving the same way I came in. Crossing the street, I look to my left. The marshal who screamed at me to "squat and cough" is sitting behind the wheel of his car, waiting for the light to turn green. He waves to me and I wave back. Like we're friends.

Reaching our car, I open the passenger door, the stress of the day apparent as Kyla collapses in the front seat. Walking around the back of the car, I pause for a moment to look at her. Question after question sprints through my mind: *What happens next? What will she say? What will I say? Will she leave me? How do I make this not my fault?*

I drive south down Route 95, weak and confused. I'm grateful we're beating the evening rush-hour traffic. I don't want to prolong this.

The silence is broken as she explains her experience. She's not looking at me and her voice is on the verge of collapse.

"They knocked on the door around 8:30—I knew something was wrong by the way they knocked: it was loud and fast. Nobody knocks like that. Matisse freaked out, jumping off the bed and running to the door, barking and growling."

I'm keeping my eyes on the road but her gaze has turned to me.

"I opened the door, trying to keep Matisse from running out, and there they were. At least fifteen of them, some kneeling, some standing—each of them pointing a gun at me.

"They told me they had a warrant for your arrest and a search warrant for the house. One of them asked where you were. I told them you went to work in the city. They handed me a piece of paper and walked past me like I wasn't even there. They went into every room and started opening closets and drawers."

I thought about our sanctuary, our safe place, the home Kyla made for us. She had to watch as it was being dissected piece by piece—our lives crumbling in front of her. There was no stopping it.

"They pointed guns at me, Craig!" she sobs. "At my face, at my chest!"

Her voice belongs to someone who's been hurt more than they knew was possible.

"You will never know what that feels like."

She's right. I hope I never will.

"You don't understand. They went through everything. Everything."

Laptops, tablets, bank statements. Everything they're looking for.

I remember I hid some routers in our condo building's closets. *No way they had a warrant for those.* A brief moment of patting myself on the back is replaced with the knowledge that it doesn't matter. They found what they needed.

I think of her bras and panties and some stranger running their hands through everything—and Kyla powerless to do anything about it.

I haven't absorbed what happened; I'm still, somehow, holding onto the hope.

"It will all be okay," I say. "We'll sort it out tomorrow."

The reality is: I know life will never be the same.

THREE

"Everything can change in an instant. Everything.
And then there is only before and after."
–PHYLLIS REYNOLDS NAYLOR

I FEEL LIKE WE'RE TRESPASSING. IT'S LIKE WE'RE WALKING into someone else's house. These homeowners have a dog and a cat just like ours, but this home belongs to the FBI. They know every inch of it, maybe better than I do. Every facet of our lives had been carefully inspected, analyzed. Violated.

The invisible security blanket that protected our home is gone now and, with it, the warmth that once occupied this space.

In its place, a cold shadow lurks.

The house isn't in chaos but things are not quite where we left them: drawers opened just a crack, clothes wrinkled, books moved. Everything is almost where it's supposed to be but not quite. It's unsettling.

Reminders of the search pop up over the next several months.

Things were missing: tax documents, old iPhones and electronics—all taken into evidence. Items were left behind, land mines we discovered one by one: evidence bags, FBI letterhead, and notes.

We went to more open houses than I can count searching for this home. We knew we found it the moment we walked through the front door. It was new construction and we would be the first to live in it. The kitchen opens to the living room, the Wolf range with its red knobs begging to be used. The master bath a sea of white Carrara marble. A guest bedroom for family and friends. Moving from our small one-bedroom, we would have more room for Kyla's growing vintage furniture business. This was the next chapter in our lives.

I fought long and hard with the bank to purchase this home. Only a short time after the mortgage crisis, the bank analyzed every minute detail of our finances. They would ask for one document, then another, then another. Each document we provided opened the door to more information being required. I should have given up this fight but I wanted to make this happen for us. I had to make it happen.

This thing I wanted so badly was now a place we couldn't stand to be.

"I hate this house," Kyla says. She speaks with the conviction of someone who has had fifteen guns pointed at her face. "I can't live here. They destroyed it."

There's nowhere we can go. We're prisoners of my actions.

I thought of my father and stepmother, Paula, the fear and

uncertainty they must be feeling. They haven't heard from us in hours.

It's time to make phone calls.

I go to our closet, shut the door, and sit on the floor. I'm like a kid hiding from his parents. These are the most difficult conversations I've ever had. Each call starts the same way: everyone excited to hear my voice, only to be brought to silence when I tell them, "I was arrested by the FBI."

My father-in-law thinks I'm playing a joke. I try to explain what happened but our phones might be bugged. I'm scared to go into too much detail.

I call my new boss, thinking of how I sneaked out of the office the moment I had walked in. "I know I've only been working with you for a short while and I thank you for the opportunity, but I have to resign effective immediately. Something has come up."

He rejects my resignation. He says to give it some time. "Whatever you're dealing with will work itself out."

It's impossible to reconcile what's happened. It's just too big and unexpected. I can't believe how far we've gone in such a short amount of time, how quickly life has changed.

That morning, as I was walking out of the door, Kyla and I played a game that we play every day. One of our rituals, all couples have them. The things that make each relationship unique. When a relationship is over, the routine is one of the things we miss the most.

Standing just inside the door, she had looked at me with pure and genuine love, as I asked, "Who's the most beautiful woman in the world?"

"Me!"

"Who's the most amazing woman in the world?"

"Me!"

"Who do I love more than anything?"

"Me!"

"Who is my favorite?"

"Me!"

Now rambling around our home, trying to get away from something that we couldn't escape, the eyes of pure and genuine love are gone. Instead, they are filled with sadness, pain, and mistrust.

It's the pain that's born when what we love has been destroyed. She looks at me like I was a dog that snapped at her once.

She says, "How could you?"

And "You lied to me."

And "You said it was okay."

She says, "What happened to our lives?"

I lied. There's nothing I can say to fix this.

The beauty of the morning recedes into memory.

FOUR

*"When you love you wish to do things for. You
wish to sacrifice for. You wish to serve."*
—ERNEST HEMINGWAY

KYLA CALLED ME, FRANTIC. "CAN YOU PLEASE COME TO
Massachusetts? I need you here. For my sanity."

We've only been dating a short time but already there's nothing
I wouldn't do for her. I pay five dollars to a man on a lawn chair
and park my car on the church lawn—the white steeple casting
a shadow across the grass. I've arrived at the Brimfield Flea
Market, one of the largest flea markets in the world. Kyla and
her aunt are here to sell furniture.

The atmosphere is frenetic, excitement and anxiety buzzing in
the air. Vendors scramble to unload their goods. Vans, cars, and
moving trucks line the streets of what would soon become a
small city.

Laid out like a NYC neighborhood—crosstown streets, north
and south avenues—the market is a perfect square grid, tent

after tent, some big and some small. Each tent is cluttered with novelties, jewelry, art, and furniture—some of it beautiful, some of it the tackiest crap I've ever seen.

We unload the moving truck; it's backbreaking work. Kyla and her aunt meticulously decorate and organize. I move things where they need to go.

We transform the white tent into a country home set in the South of France. Shades of white and pastels contrast with darker colors: there is a depth to the space. If it weren't a tent in the middle of a flea market, I'd live here.

With the hard work done, Kyla and I set off to explore. The sun shines through the wisps of clouds in the otherwise clear, blue sky. Her hair turns the brightest of yellow when the wind catches it just right.

I stare into her eyes, where gold flecks float in a sea of green, reflecting in the sun.

She's been going to flea markets her entire life. They're a family tradition. She has the passion and fire of someone speaking about their life's purpose but they haven't discovered it yet.

Something grabs her attention and she runs to it: a gray, wooden corbel that was saved from demolition, an industrial drafting desk dating back to the early twentieth century. Her slender fingers trace their outline as she says, "You would use this in this way, or this would go there. This would make a great dining room table…"

I know nothing about this world she loves, but it doesn't matter.

I could listen all day. One thought keeps popping into my mind: *She's the most beautiful woman I've ever seen.*

We walk for hours, side by side, speaking, listening, laughing, and sharing. She reaches for my hand. Those long, elegant fingers intertwine with mine, our palms touch. As if a circuit has been completed, a surge of electricity lights me up. I smile as I realize this is the first time we've held hands. We continue to walk and talk, hand in hand.

She lets go when a dresser, desk, or anything catches her eye and she runs to it. I love how she reaches for my hand the moment she's once again by my side.

The sky turns a brilliant orange and red, signals it's time for me to leave. We walk to my car. The guy is still in his lawn chair.

We kiss under the shadow of the church steeple, our lips coming together gently and softly. It's the kiss of new beginnings and possibilities.

Driving home, my hands wrapped around the wheel, the electricity of her fingers linger in mine.

I'm in love.

FIVE

"The human heart is like a night bird. Silently waiting for something, and when the time comes, it flies straight toward it."
—HARUKI MURAKAMI

WE'RE SITTING ON OUR SOFA, BATHED IN WHITE CHRIST-mas lights. Her leg draped over mine, a glass of wine in hand. The wooden beams and air-conditioning ducts of our loft cast shadows on the wall.

Growing up, my father filled our family room with giant Christmas trees. The soaring ceilings of our new apartment meant we were lucky enough to have one of our own. Some people take the easy way with Christmas lights, draping them around the tree. Others meticulously wrap each individual branch, giving the tree the depth of a star-filled night sky.

Kyla is a wrapper.

Midnight quickly approaches; Christmas day will soon be yes-terday. I know what I want to do. I'm prepared. The moment is as close to perfect as it's going to get. I make my move. As I fall to the ground, I realize I did not prepare for the slippery leather sofa. I recover, not so gracefully, and get on one knee.

I didn't rehearse and I didn't need to.

"You are the most incredible, amazing, beautiful woman in the world. Every time I look at you, you grow even more beautiful. You are my favorite and I love you more than anything. I'm a better man because of you and my life is better because of you. I want to spend the rest of my life with you. Will you marry me?"

I know the answer before she even opens her smiling mouth. The tears forming in her eyes give her away. I don't know if it's the light of the tree, but she's glowing.

She reaches for my hands. "Yes, I'll marry you," she squeals, hopping up and down like a child who just heard Santa's sleigh.

I hold her face in my palm, wiping a tear away with my thumb. She extends her left hand, and I carefully slide my grandmother's ring onto her delicate finger. A few sizes too big, it doesn't matter. She holds her hand in front of her, the facets glistening in the light. She reaches for her phone and calls everyone she can—no hello, no Merry Christmas. The second she hears a voice on the other side, she screams with delight, "I'm getting married!"

Initially, we wanted a big ceremony, a hundred-plus guests, maybe a destination wedding. But after lots of work and planning, the magic gets sucked out of the moment. One night over wine, we discuss our wedding plans, the fact that neither of us was in love with them. Too much money, too much planning, too much work—we only want to be with those closest to us. We only want to be with each other.

We arrange the wedding in thirty days and have the ceremony on November 5, the same day Marty McFly arrives in Hill Valley (a coincidence I take great joy in). We're blown away by the staff's dedication to making this happen. They keep the restaurant, Gabriel's in Greenwich, CT, open later than usual to accommodate us. In a complete violation of health codes, they allow Matisse in the ceremony.

Our florist made a flower dog collar for her. It looked beautiful for all of ten seconds before Matisse turned it into a toy. We laugh as my father wrestles with Matisse in a valiant effort to fix her collar.

We gather in the main dining room, the guests facing the ivory fireplace covered in decorations. My best friends standing by my side, I look out at our family and friends. Love, joy, and excitement in their eyes. For too long, I'd been wrapped up in making money. It dictated my life.

I ignored my family, holding petty grievances that served no purpose other than an excuse not to spend time with them. Kyla made it a point to change that.

Months before the wedding we visited North Carolina to spend time with my mother, lunches with my father and Paula. Trips to see Aunt Bobbi. Driving halfway across the country to support her father in a marathon, trips to California to spend time with her cousin, Lauren. She made all this possible through her generosity, her love, her caring, her knowledge of what's essential.

Everyone here and the relationships cultivated, a product of Kyla's love.

With the sound of a single guitar string, everyone's attention turns to the back of the room. The restaurant manager, the man who made all this possible in thirty days, opens a set of double doors. There is a collective gasp when they see her: her smile is so big, it would hurt your face to replicate it. Holding a bouquet of white peonies, Kyla and her father, complete in his Air Force service dress, slowly walk down the aisle. If anyone has ever looked more beautiful, I'd like to see it. I don't believe it's possible.

Tom Wait's distinct voice, singing, "I want you, you, you; all I want is you, you, you..."

The room grows quiet, the justice of the peace delivers his lines as we hold hands and stare into each other's eyes. It's time for our vows. She unfolds a piece of paper, her gentle voice reciting the words of Walt Whitman:

> "Camerado, I give you my hand!
> I give you my love more precious than money,
> I give you myself before preaching or law;
> Will you give me yourself? Will you come travel with me?
> Shall we stick by each other as long as we live?"

I promise to bring her tea in bed every morning, movies, cheese plates, and wine on rainy days. This is the only wedding I've been to with audience participation; my aunt chimes in, "I want that too!" and everyone laughs and agrees.

The justice of the peace finishes the ceremony with the words everyone at a wedding waits for: "I now pronounce you man and wife. You may kiss the bride."

Everyone stands and claps as we kiss and walk down the aisle.

The manager of the restaurant opens the door to a private dining room. "Take a moment by yourselves," he says. "Enjoy this for all it's worth."

We duck into the room as he closes the door behind us. We embrace, we kiss, we wipe the tears from each other's cheeks. She takes hold of my left hand, her fingers gently touching my wedding band. "Do you like it?"

"I love it. It's beautiful."

She smiles like someone with a delicious secret. "Take it off. Look inside."

I slide the ring off my finger, tilting it to the light so I can see. My heart swells and tears fill my eyes as I read the words engraved in beautiful cursive: *You are my favorite.*

Nothing I own, no expensive watches or cars, is as valuable to me as this ring and its message. We hold each other for a moment longer before joining the party. I didn't know it was possible to feel this much love and joy.

While our guests enjoy the cocktail hour, we go outside for pictures. It's a beautiful fall day, a far cry from the blizzard that swept the Northeast the weekend before. We were afraid flights would be canceled and, in turn, the wedding.

We walk, hand in hand, down the tree-lined avenue. The leaves crunching beneath our feet. An SUV screeches to a halt in the middle of the street, a car full of young girls, no more than eleven years old, run toward us as though they've found the world's only unicorn.

They all speak at the same time. We have no idea what is going on. One of their fathers manages to get a word in through the chaos. They're in the middle of a scavenger hunt, competing against other teams. One of the items to scavenge for? A bride and groom.

"Can we please have a picture with you?!"

"Please!"

"We're going to win for sure!"

"You're so beautiful! I love your dress!"

We're honored to be a part of their hunt. As the SUV pulls away, we look at each other, both of us agreeing, "They're going to win this thing."

We're thirty-two people in total. The sweeping staircases frame the four round tables and fireplace. Fall is on full display. Pumpkins and birch branches fill the room.

These are the people who matter. Only the closest, most important people in our lives. I can't imagine doing it any other way. It feels right.

The maid of honor speaks. I'm fortunate to have two best men, both delivering beautiful speeches. The evening transforms into an open-mic night. Almost all of the guests speak, everyone jumping at the opportunity to grab the microphone.

Before the wedding, we were given a piece of advice from a married couple we had met: "Throughout the evening of your wedding, stop, take a breath, and look at where you are and what you are doing. Do this throughout the night. It will go so fast and will seem like a blur. Take time to create memories."

I remembered those words, stopping occasionally and taking it all in. I watch Kyla talk to our family and friends and people dancing and laughing. This is truly one of the best nights of my life.

The night comes to an end. Exhausted, thrilled, overwhelmed, we climb into bed. I hold her in my arms, watching as she drifts off to sleep. I hold my hand up, look at my ring, as I kiss the top of her head, whispering, "You are my favorite."

SIX

"You can't conquer reality by running away from it."
–OG MANDINO

IN THE SEVEN WEEKS SINCE MY ARREST, THAT COUPLE has all but vanished. Staring at my ring, I think of the words engraved inside. I'm only beginning to understand what I've lost.

I leave the comfort of the sofa and walk into the kitchen. I sit in the same spot every night, my back resting against the cabinet between the refrigerator and stove—the sound of the fridge humming in my ear. A rocks glass in my right hand, my fingers damp from the condensation—a bottle of Captain Morgan within reach.

She went to sleep hours ago. I hope sleep provides the reprieve she deserves—a reprieve from me, from the uncertainty, from life. I stay up, sometimes for hours, alone with my thoughts and the bottle.

I've developed a nice trick to convince myself I'm in control. I pour just a little into the glass. Quarter pours, over and over again. Watching as the rum carves its way through the ice. I love the sound of the ice melting. I love the ceremony of it all. The quarter pours add up, the empty bottle at the end of the night never lies.

The truth is emerging and I want to drown it. I want to kill it before it kills me. It's always there, running in the background. I choose to ignore it. I can't ignore it any longer. I'm sitting on the kitchen floor by myself, drowning myself in rum.

There were signs. I pretended not to see them. They were so obvious, the universe and everyone around me screaming at me to stop. Kyla asked me on an almost daily basis, "Are you sure this is okay?"

I was pissed she was questioning me. My anger hid how scared I was by the truth.

My accountant told me, "This doesn't sound right to me. Craig, you're operating in a very grey area."

I was pissed at him too.

I lost my best friend, Rob, the co-best man at the wedding, all because of what I'd become: an angry, scared man, hiding behind lies and the things I could buy. Rob couldn't take my arrogance or how I treated him.

"Hey, you've changed," he told me, "and I don't like who you've become or how I feel about myself when I'm around you. You've hurt my feelings. I'm going to pull back from our friendship."

Whatever. I was newly married and in love. He was the one who'd changed and I had filled the void.

I wish I could protect myself from myself.

My back hurts from leaning against the cabinet. I bend my knees and rest my elbows on them to take some of the pressure off. Taking a sip, the rum tickles the back of my throat as I flashback to walking into the UPS store to pick up another package. The awkward exchanges with the clerks exacerbate my guilt and shame.

"Pick up for box forty-nine."

"Uh-huh, so what do you do anyway? You have your own business?"

I hated this question. I hated that they all smelled like week-old cigarettes and cardboard.

"I do."

"What do you do?"

"Tech sales."

I felt as though they all knew I was doing something shady. I longed for the safety of my car, away from the smell and the guilt. The scent would linger in my nose for a while. The guilt never left.

Sitting on the floor, I try to drink the memories away, but they won't stop.

I think of the afternoon my heart screamed at me like it was the last chance it would ever have to scream. I had just put a load of laundry into the washer. A number, out of nowhere, popped into my mind. It was as loud and clear as it was sad: *One. Million. Dollars.*

I broke the million-dollar mark that week. What I did couldn't be changed and that realization froze me in fear. I had no choice but to lie to myself. *It's okay. It will work itself out the way it always does.*

I was praying for something beyond myself to make it stop. I didn't know how to stop this thing I had started without something else ending it for me. Thankfully, I did get that new job. I wasn't going to jeopardize this opportunity. Without that or the arrest, I don't know how long I would have continued.

As I sip the rum, the truth is quicksand. The more I fight it, the more it engulfs me.

I'm a good drinker, always have been. I can out-drink people twice my size. The first time I got drunk was in the sixth grade and I never really stopped. I loved the escape that alcohol provides—the freedom to be someone else for a few hours.

Here on the kitchen floor, there is no freedom, only the false promise of it. Every night starts the same, teasing me with dreams of escape: the warmth of the rum over the chill of ice. Delicious. The feeling that life, the truth, the overwhelming burden, would fade.

I can live a life other than my own.

Every night I follow the siren's song and every night it betrays me. I can't escape reality. The alcohol only exaggerates it. Questions run in circles in my mind.

Why did I do this to my life?

What have I done to the woman I love?

Why didn't I stop?

Why didn't I listen to the voice inside?

I'm drinking too much. My brain is deteriorating. Memories are missing. I'm dull and slow. Normal daily activities—loading the dishwasher, folding clothes, checking emails—are a struggle. I can't put ideas together. I feel inadequate that I can't function like I once did. Inadequacy leads to depression, missing memories leads to paranoia.

I see who I really am. I know what I'm capable of. I can't trust myself. How can I trust anyone else? People are out to get me. The FBI is hiding in every black SUV; every conversation is being recorded.

Is Kyla cheating on me?

The interactions of daily life are a struggle. I'm convinced everyone I interact with knows I'm a criminal: gas station attendants, deli clerks, bank tellers, everyone. I'm wearing a scarlet letter only I can see.

I look at their left ear or a spot on the wall behind them. I can't let anyone look me in the eye. I'm a shadow everyone sees through.

Living in my brain is hell. I'm worthless.

I arrive at the same conclusion every night, my life insurance policy. The financial disclosure I completed for the government, every penny earned, everything I own—it's all right there. The numbers don't lie; I'm worth more dead than alive. My life insurance policy would fix everything. I consider the logistics.

Did I pay the insurance bill? Is there a suicide clause? If so, what does it say? Is there a way around it? The money has to make it to Kyla, my sister, my niece, and my nephew.

Think of what she could do with the money. She could escape this hell and live a life of freedom. Her business would flourish. My sister and brother-in-law would have financial security, the kid's college tuition paid for.

It sounded nice but I never actually read the insurance policy. I was afraid of what I would find. She would get the money or she wouldn't. Either option was terrible. If she were guaranteed the money, that meant I would have to kill myself. If she wouldn't get the money, killing myself is a waste—a selfish act with no reward.

I destroyed my life and beg for it to be anything other than it is—the damage done, the unknown future, the total mistrust in myself—but it's the same climax.

I think about Kyla waking up in the morning to an empty bed, wondering where I am, walking to the kitchen to find me on the floor in a puddle of my sadness and snot. I couldn't bear the embarrassment and shame. I pull myself off the floor, clean the puddle, and pass out in bed.

Only to do it all over again tomorrow night.

SEVEN

*"All human things hang on a slender thread, the
strongest fall with a sudden crash."*

−OVID

THE MORE KYLA AND I TRY TO LIVE A NORMAL LIFE, THE
more apparent it becomes that our lives are far from normal.
But we do try. We have to, for our sanity.

It's Christmas Eve and we're doing what we do every Christmas
Eve. We're celebrating at Dad and Paula's, or at least pretending
to. It feels good to be out of the house with people other than
ourselves. This is a much-needed reprieve from reality, even if
it's only for a few hours.

We're sitting in the living room, the white lights reflecting off
the gold and silver ornaments on perhaps the most symmetrical
Christmas tree in the world. The children squeal with joy as
they open their presents—the smell and sound of the fireplace.
This is a moment of light in our world of darkness.

Dad and Paula hand us our present, a bright red envelope. We open it and pull out the card. The yellow Lab in a Santa hat makes me smile. We always get each other cards with dogs, an unspoken family tradition.

Tears fill our eyes when we see the check inside. I think Kyla's are out of joy. Mine are fueled by shame. Their generosity strikes at the center of my unworthiness. We cry as we hug, the rest of the family looking slightly confused as to what is happening.

It makes me think of my entire family, their love and support. I'm grateful for them. I know how fortunate I am. I also know their kindness burns.

It's time to leave but I don't want to. Even though I'm swimming in shame, I want to stay here. I'm protected from the real world. I'm not ready to go back yet. But we have to.

Driving south through Bridgeport, a gentle drizzle starts falling from the sky. People hope for a white Christmas, but this is not it. It's cold, raw, and wet.

We're talking about how incredible they are, how that really was the most symmetrical Christmas tree in the world.

I ask, "Do you think he pruned it to be that perfect? Or did they find it that way?"

The windshield wipers create a soothing sense of calm as we speak. Without warning, the back end of the car breaks free. We're sliding across four lanes of traffic at sixty-five miles per hour. The seemingly harmless drizzle has transformed the highway into a sheet of black ice.

I'm fighting the steering wheel as we cross the highway. The car topples sideways as we careen back and forth. Kyla's screams fill my ears. My body's taken over and is acting without me thinking.

Miraculously, I regain control of the car. The helpless back and forth has stopped. I slowly ease into the right-hand lane, dropping to a comfortable twenty-five miles per hour.

Disaster averted. I glue my eyes to the white line on our right. The white line is my friend. It will get us to safety.

My heartbeat is slowing; my breath is returning to normal. The adrenaline is draining from my veins. We're going to be okay. I look at the surrounding area and think of the miles still ahead of us. We're only in Bridgeport. Home feels like an eternity away. I must get us home, that's all I have to do. I thought, *Just get us home, off of 95. It will be safer once we hit Greenwich.*

I take my eyes off the road just for a second to look at her. She looks into my eyes and says, "I thought we were going to die."

The driver's side window explodes in a violent fury of glass, metal, and plastic. My face and neck sting as pieces of the window hit them like shrapnel. I didn't see the pickup truck. He lost control precisely as we had.

We spin out of control. Inertia has taken over. The headlights of oncoming traffic blind us as we slide across the highway. I think, *Why am I seeing headlights right now? Why are they all aiming at us? Is that an eighteen-wheeler? We're going the wrong way.*

I don't see the pickup truck coming the second time either, as it crashes into the driver's side. Her screams are louder than the crash. Frantically I stab at the brakes and turn the wheel, fighting against what I don't know.

With no control, I'm consumed by helplessness as we collide head-on into the center median. The silence after a violent accident is the sound of our brains catching up to what just happened.

I sit in the silence for five seconds or maybe five minutes. I'm alone in my mind.

I did this to us. This is another punishment for what I did. I don't think I can take anymore.

My brain catches up, the sound of glass trickling to the ground, the radiator hissing as coolant pours out of it. I turn to her. "Are you okay?"

"I'm okay." She takes a deep breath. "Are you?"

"I'm okay."

I try to open my door, but it won't budge. I have to climb out of the passenger side. My back tells me I might not be okay. I keep my mouth shut and deal with it.

I check on the truck driver and his passenger. Everyone's alive; everyone is okay. Minus my back, which is speaking louder with every second. It's a miracle no one was seriously injured—an absolute miracle.

Kyla and I do not embrace. We don't share our relief; we keep to ourselves. Processing, or at least trying to, what happened on our own. We do not look into each other's eyes and say, "I love you."

We stand side by side on this rainy Christmas Eve as strangers. Inches away. Miles apart. The damage done.

Not by the truck, not by the ice. By a break in trust.

EIGHT

"He declares himself guilty who justifies himself before accusation."
–PROVERB

"HOW DOES THE DEFENDANT PLEAD?"

Everyone in the courtroom is waiting on my answer. It's why we're all here: the judge, the prosecutor, the FBI, my attorney, and me.

I didn't want Kyla to be here and she didn't want to come. I didn't want her to hear me say what I'm about to say. What everyone in the courtroom is waiting for me to say. I know it's over. I know the three words that I must speak. It doesn't mean I want to. I don't have much choice in the matter. My attorney made it clear that there were no other options. I would be pleading guilty to the charge of mail fraud.

In our meetings leading to this moment, I tried several times to explain to my attorney how the government was wrong. "This sentence they wrote is not accurate," I had insisted. "I did return the components to the manufacturer."

"Doesn't matter. You will lose."

Even at the opposite end of the conference table, his six-foot frame looms over me. His dark eyes and stern expression tell me he is not messing around. *Did he go grey from stress or from age?*

He speaks deliberately and without emotion. "The government doesn't like it when people fight. Especially when they know, they are right. The government doesn't like trials. They cost them time and money. When you're inevitably found guilty, they'll sentence you to the maximum they can. They will punish you for bringing this to trial."

That didn't sound right to me, but the fear it instilled outweighed my sense of right and wrong. I was picking at the smallest of details, missing the big picture. The fact is, I did use my extensive knowledge of the victim's warranty policy to secure brand-new pieces of networking equipment that I later sold at a profit. I was fighting over grains of sand on a beach.

My attorney reiterated, "You will lose. If you plea, you have a shot at probation. Which I cannot guarantee, but for the offense you committed, it sounds reasonable."

That is why I am standing in this courtroom now, on this cold January day. I open my mouth to speak. My voice is shaky. I don't want to say it. The moment I do, I'm immediately a federally convicted felon. But I have to; I have to take a shot.

"Guilty, Your Honor."

I feel like I made a mistake. I feel like my life is over.

The judge nods her head in approval. "The court accepts your plea; you will be sentenced on June 10, 2014. Let the record show that the defendant made an unusual and exceptional immediate payment of $100,000 in restitution."

I had closed my 401(k) to do this. Kyla asked me not to, but I moved ahead regardless. I wanted to buy myself into a better sentence or no sentence at all. I made a $100,000 bet that will or will not come to fruition in five months.

In less than one second, I'm a convicted felon. I will carry this moniker for the remainder of my life. My life is cast in the shadow of an unknown future and there is not a thing I can do about it.

NINE

FOR MONTHS, WE'VE BEEN LIVING LIVES THAT ARE NOT our own. They belong to the people working on my sentencing. Some I've met, others I may never meet. I'm just a criminal to them. Whoever I may be as a person doesn't really matter. It's a crappy feeling and I know it's true: I am a criminal. I pled guilty.

Neither of us can predict the future but every potential outcome is terrible. My fantasy scenario is three years of probation, a court order barring me from the tech industry, losing all our assets, and paying restitution for the remainder of my life. I'm banking everything on this. The thought of prison makes me nauseous. I think of my 120-pound frame and how easily I could be beaten and raped.

June 10, 2014, is casting a shadow over our lives.

We spend our days preparing for the future. Her business is the only way I know how to keep a roof over our heads, particularly her head since there is a real chance I'll go to prison. Our relationship has been reduced to survival and the overwhelming stress that accompanies the need to survive.

She continues to ask the same questions because I continue to avoid them:

"How could you?"

"Why did you lie to me?"

"What happened to our lives?"

I'm afraid to answer them. I'm scared to admit I was wrong and I couldn't give up the need to be right. I'm scared to admit that I ignored the voice inside, the increasing awareness that I did this because I was scared to ask life for what I really wanted.

I invested too much at this point in being right. I can't back down. I'm fighting with her and myself. I know I'm wrong. Everything inside me tells me I am, my heart, my life, all screaming at me. I'm just too afraid to confront the truth. No wonder I try to escape every night.

It's easier to convince myself that she's upset because our lifestyle was taken from us—the dinners, the expensive dresses and shoes. I keep thinking, *Why is she so worried about anything? She's beautiful, smart, gifted. She's creating this business that's going to flourish—with or without me. I'm the one going to prison. I'm the one who lost everything. She'll be just fine. I'm the victim here…I did this for her.*

After a long day of moving furniture, exhausted and vulnerable, another argument erupts. I don't have the strength to admit I'm wrong. I'm digging my heels in more and more. I'm angry at her anger. *How dare she get this upset at me. The only reason she feels this way is her fear of losing the lifestyle I gave us.*

I'm blind to what was in front of me.

Sitting on the very edge of our sofa, barely holding on, she looks at me with tear-filled eyes and says the words that bring me down with the same impact as the voicemail from the FBI, "I'm sad because my dreams for us have been destroyed!"

Instantly, I know what she means—our conversation in the bedroom, our second chance. The dreams we shared, the life we wanted to build. None of it revolved around things but experiences. The creation of a life we'd both love, hand in hand, as husband and wife, lovers, and best friends. This had nothing to do with dresses, shoes, or dinners. It had to do with reconnecting with who we are and whom we fell in love with. We could have been poor as long as we were moving forward together.

I'm speechless. Who the fuck have I become?

She breaks the silence. "I'm not writing a letter."

Every time I think I hit bottom, I discover another level of hell.

As part of a defendant's defense, we're allowed to provide character letters written by our spouses, family, and friends. Defendants are strangers to the judge. We never meet. They don't know anything about us other than the information the prosecutor provides. These letters are a window into our lives, of who we are outside of the charges we face. Some lawyers argue these letters are the most crucial piece of evidence a defendant can provide.

"I don't want them twisting my words around," she says. "They'll manipulate whatever I say."

I believe her fear is genuine. I also think she's so severely hurt that she can't find the words.

My family, friends, and neighbors had been submitting their letters over the last couple of weeks and I was so grateful. But without Kyla's support, I have nothing.

I'm such a piece of shit, my own wife won't write a letter on my behalf.

Standing in our living room, there was nothing I could say. I've discovered who I am, and I despise what I see.

TEN

"Nobody ever did, or ever will, escape the consequences of his choices."
–ALFRED A. MONTAPERT

THE SHADOW NOW HAS A FACE. THE FEDERAL COURT-house in New Haven, Connecticut. A massive building, imposing in its size, and the knowledge that my fate will be decided within its walls. We walk up the granite steps and through the heavy doors. Nine months of uncertainty distilled to this moment.

My family and friends are already here. It feels like walking into a wake. They speak softly and with condolences. I watch as my family and friends say hello to one another. Some of them are meeting for the first time; it's embarrassing that this is the setting. Everyone cast in the shadow, everyone doing their best to remain positive.

I am surrounded by people who love me and support me and yet I feel so alone. I want to shrink and disappear. I want to escape the shame and unworthiness their love is illuminating.

Standing in the hallway just outside the courtroom, I decide to walk over to the creepy FBI agent to extend a "Hey, no hard feelings" handshake. He seems indifferent about it. A representative for the victim is sitting with the agents. As I walk away, I overhear the agents ask him, "So, is this a big case for you guys?"

"Nah, this is nothing."

Great, I think, *I destroyed our lives, and I'm not even a blip on their radar.*

A voice echoes through the marble hallway, "Now calling The United States vs. Craig Stanland."

Panic tears through my body as we file into the courtroom. My wife, family, and friends take their seats in the gallery behind me. The "United States" sits across the aisle.

I look around the massive room with soaring ceilings and no soul. It's purposeful and deliberate in its design—a government room in a government building. I don't know if the room is cold or if it's nerves, but I'm freezing.

My gaze goes to the cameras on the walls, one on each side of the room. They're pointed right at me. I imagine this is being livestreamed to the world. *Are they on? I wonder. Please don't be on; I'm embarrassed enough; I don't need this recorded...*

My heart, tired of being ignored, has deserted me. Locked deep inside my body, not willing to come out, the hole in the middle of my chest is eating me alive. My fate, my life, my future is on the line.

The judge enters the room, and we're ordered to rise. She walks deliberately, eventually taking her place on the bench. After we sit down, the prosecutor begins outlining the charges against me.

"From approximately October 2012 to the current date, Mr. Stanland committed fraud against the victim, using his position and vast knowledge of the company's policies to his illicit gain.

"Specifically, Mr. Stanland operated a service contract fraud scheme in which he purchased or controlled approximately eighteen service contracts for the victim's networking parts.

"Pursuant to these service contracts, Mr. Stanland—using the aliases 'Alan Johnston' of Opex Solutions, 'Kyle Booker' of KLB Networks, 'Steve Jones' of SHO Networks, 'Robert Johnson' of Adaptations, 'Paul Smith' of PS Solutions, among others—made hundreds of false service requests to the victim to replace purportedly defective computer networking parts.

"Based on these requests, the victim shipped replacement parts to various addresses at Mr. Stanland's direction, including to his home in Stamford; to his wife's business in Brooklyn, New York; and to two post office boxes in Greenwich, Connecticut.

"Mr. Stanland sold the new parts to third parties to enrich himself.

"Through this scheme, Mr. Stanland fraudulently obtained nearly 600 parts from the victim.

"In one month alone, Mr. Stanland profited $28,000."

There is a gasp from the gallery, my mother's voice rising above all the others.

The prosecutor's mission is to paint the defendant in an unflattering light, highlighting the greed and corruption. The government subpoenaed restaurants we went to, obtaining receipts from our meals.

"On April 20, 2013, Mr. Stanland went to Polpo restaurant, located in Greenwich, Connecticut, where he ordered the octopus appetizer, the spaghetti Bolognese, tiramisu for dessert, and a bottle of Purple Angel wine. The total cost of the meal: $236.54."

He repeated this exercise for several restaurants, reinforcing the lavish lifestyle I was living on ill-gotten gains. I'm surprised and grateful that the government missed some of the really expensive meals. The judge interjects with a joke about the crash course in wine she received from the subpoenas. Only one half of the courtroom laughs.

I wonder, *How long were they onto me? What have they seen?*

I feel violated. In a moment of clarity, I understood what the manager of a restaurant was telling me. He tried to warn me. "It's crazy what the FBI will do, asking for receipts for people's meals. What are they looking for?"

I was too self-involved to hear what he was saying then.

The prosecutor finishes his piece and hands it over to a representative of the victim, the tenth-largest technology company in the world. He's a member of the fraud detection team, a team formed explicitly because of people like me. He outlines in excruciating detail the fraud I committed, dates and times, phone calls, emails, dollar amounts. He's got his information down pat.

The government rests its case. It's our turn. My attorney delivers his opening statement.

"It's not as though Mr. Stanland walked into a store and put a gun to someone's face. His computer was his weapon, a non-violent weapon…"

As he speaks, his hand makes the universal sign for a gun, pointing it and waving it around. I watch in disbelief as he continues to compare me to a violent criminal. I'm thinking, *This is what you came up with? How is this a good defense? Can you please stop referring to my computer as a weapon? Can you stop saying I used a weapon? Why are you even using the word weapon?*

I remain quiet as I imagine my attorney locking the prison cell behind me. *I spent $15,000 on this?* Finally, he finishes. I'm not sure how much longer I could listen to this crap. It's time for my family and friends to speak in my defense.

My father was chosen to speak on behalf of the family; an attorney for close to fifty years, they agreed he was the best choice. The judge addresses him directly, extending professional courtesy and respect for his law degree. She's empathetic to his circumstance.

"Mr. Stanland, this must be very difficult for you as an attorney, appearing in this courtroom about to speak on behalf of your son."

He speaks in a soft yet deliberate tone. It's a bittersweet moment, his love and support interwoven with disappointment at what his only son had done.

"Your Honor, this is the most terrible day of my life. My son is a good man; he is a good son, nephew, and uncle. He made a terrible mistake…"

He asks the judge to consider the good I've done, to extend leniency. My shame grows with every word.

I've been dreading this day, but now was the time that scared me the most. It's my turn to speak. I have an opportunity to accept responsibility and ask for leniency—a last-ditch effort to save myself. Public speaking is my biggest fear. The weight of my life rests on my shoulders.

My attorney advised me to wear the cheapest, ugliest black shoes I could find—a ploy to demonstrate that I'm a regular guy who wears regular footwear. I bought the most inexpensive pair I could find at Target, and now I'm paying for it. They've completely destroyed my feet and my back. I try to hide my limp as I walk to the podium. I look at the judge on the other side of the room and the table hiding my feet. I'm not sure how this is an effective strategy.

As per my lawyer's instructions, I prepared a statement structured in a clear and concise format that he provided. I remove it from my pocket and carefully unfold it. I focus on the public speaking advice from a friend that I'd written in big block letters on the top: SLOW DOWN.

My attorney told me not to address the crime itself but to speak in generalities. "There is not a day that goes by that I do not feel sorrow for what I have done. I accept responsibility for my actions and ask the court for leniency…"

The statement felt rote to me, bullet points instead of authenticity, very robotic in its structure. One. Two. Three. My attorney thought it was excellent. I hated it.

Both sides of the aisle have spoken. I don't know what comes next. I think about Kyla and the character letter, how she changed her mind this morning.

"I emailed my letter to Eugene," she told me. "I didn't know what to say. I don't forgive you and I'm still afraid they're going to twist my words around. But I didn't think it would look good for you if I didn't write one."

I was elated until I was told we missed the deadline—another level of hell. Even though I had Kyla's support, the judge would never see it. And neither would I.

As crucial as these letters are, I never saw any of them. My attorney requested they be sent directly to him. He never shared their contents and neither did the prosecution.

The judge announced we would be taking a short recess. She would be meeting with my pre-trial probation officer to review the evidence and render her decision, adding the comment, "Let the record show I will allow the last-minute submission of the defendant's wife's character letter after the deadline."

The judge's deprecating tone eclipses my moment of joy. *She knows Kyla thinks I'm a piece of shit.*

I don't know how long the judge was in her chambers. My future rests on what's happening in that room. It all comes down to this.

The chamber door opens. The back of my throat burns with bile.

The court officer announces, "Please rise." She enters the courtroom, holding my case file.

As the judge takes her seat, the court officer addresses the court. "All but the defendant may be seated."

I'm at the edge of a cliff, waiting to take a step back or be pushed into the abyss.

The judge opens the case file and begins. "In the case of The United States vs. Craig Stanland, on one count of mail fraud…"

I can't understand what she's saying. The words are in English, but I don't understand any of it. I can't even grasp the context. Only bits and pieces make it through. She holds the letters of support in the air, saying, "Mr. Stanland, these letters show a good man. Your friends and family care for you very much. They think you are a great man. Personally, I think you are Dr. Jekyll and Mr. Hyde, hiding behind the good you do to perform the bad."

She's right, I think.

She continues to speak a barrage of legalese, none of it registering. I'm stuck on the comparison she made: "Dr. Jekyll and Mr. Hyde." *She sees through me.*

It's all I can do to maintain consciousness. I've lost over thirty pounds from stress. I weigh five pounds less than the day I graduated high school twenty-three years ago. Being this thin is wreaking havoc on my body. I continue to regret these cheap shoes.

I'm alone; I'm terrified; I want this to be over.

The gavel comes down, echoing through the room. I don't know what happened. I turn to my attorney and ask, "Was I just sentenced to prison?"

He tilts his head to the side like a confused dog. "You were sentenced to pay $834,037 in restitution and serve twenty-four months in federal prison."

I nod. It's all I can do.

The judge adds one last statement as the gallery begins to stand and the attorneys gather their papers, "I guess we'll find out who you really are when you get out."

ELEVEN

*"Of all the words of mice and men, the
saddest are, 'It might have been.'"*
—KURT VONNEGUT

TWO YEARS IN FEDERAL PRISON. TWO YEARS AWAY FROM
her. Two years lost. The rest of my life changed forever.

We walk out of the courtroom, back to the cavernous hallway.
My friends and family extend their condolences. Everyone tries
to maintain a brave face, trying to mask the reality of what just
happened. They offer their support.

"It's going to be okay."

"Whatever we can do to help."

"We're here for both of you."

Everyone's being incredible and I hate it. I hate that I need
their support. I don't know how I would survive without it but
it hurts.

We say our goodbyes and walk to the car. The world feels different. It's like I'm no longer connected to anything. I'm alone in a bubble. I can see everything but I have no connection to anything. Alone. Scared. Isolated.

We drive home in silence, down the same stretch of Route 95 we traveled after the arrest, the same piece of road where we crashed. This road has too many bad memories. I don't know what two years of prison means. I can't wrap my head around it. I think about us and the damage I've done. I hope and pray she'll be there when I get out. I hope we can start over.

Arriving home, the house is emptier than after the FBI search. Since I owe restitution, it's no longer our home. It belongs to the government and Wells Fargo. I'm living on borrowed time in someone else's house.

I expected a form of closure from knowing my fate. Living in uncertainty for the last ten months has been soul crushing. Even if it were the worst possible outcome, I thought it would help to know. It doesn't. I'm as lost as ever.

We walk into our bedroom, stripping off our courtroom clothes. I want these damn shoes off. Kyla is still asking the same questions because I still refuse to answer them honestly.

"How could you do this to us?"

"What have you done?"

"We're not going to have sex for two years?"

"What are we going to do for two years?"

"How are we going to survive?"

Even now, with the finality of my prison sentence staring me in the face, I fight to be right. Maybe I'm trying to preserve the last thing I think I have left: being right.

I've been ordered to report to Otisville Federal Prison on August 13, 2014, no later than 12 p.m. We have two months to plan and prepare for the next two years, as if life follows a plan.

We scramble to figure out priorities, what needs to be done first. How does one figure what to take care of now so that the next two years will be okay?

There are too many balls in the air—our home, the mortgage, taxes to file, bills, closing accounts, credit cards, car leases, passwords to bank accounts, and every other service we use.

She can't afford to live in our house. We have to find her an apartment, then find a tenant for the condo. We have a year's worth of work and a two-month window.

The shame and guilt I feel for what I've done to her are coming to a head. I want nothing more than to make sure she has what she needs to survive for the next two years.

Her business is just starting to do well. We rented a showroom on the second floor of an industrial warehouse, very cool, very Brooklyn. The space is incredible, what she fills it with even more so, but without a storefront, foot traffic is minimal. For her to survive, to keep a roof over her head, the business has to grow.

And we didn't know how to do it.

Taking a break from the showroom, we walk down the neighborhood's main street, looking for a bite to eat. This is her dream street. In a perfect world, this is where she would set up shop. As if the universe heard her prayer, we see it. An empty store, a sign in the window: "Available for -pop-up shops. Short term, as little as one week."

We cup our hands around our eyes and press our faces up to the glass. It's incredible: hardwood floors, high tin ceilings, giant windows, natural light streaming in, a brick fireplace.

She says, "Is that an apartment in the back? Could we live here?"

This is it. This is what we need. We can rent it for a week and dip our toes into what it would be like to have a storefront. Both of us are excited but scared it would be nothing more than a pipe dream. Was it too much money? What's the catch? We contact the landlord. This isn't a pipe dream; there is no catch.

Long before the arrest, my mother came for a visit. She spent the day in the showroom with us, cleaning and dusting all the furniture—classic rock playing through the vintage stereo, a whisper of static adding to the atmosphere. My mother danced and cleaned simultaneously, greeting customers as they walked in. It was one of the happiest I've ever seen my mother. She still glows when she talks about it. We tell her about the pop-up shop and she generously volunteers to pay the fee.

The store is ours for a week.

Truckload after truckload, we transfer everything from the showroom to the store in addition to buying more. The work is hard, long days, nonstop. In two days, we transform the once-empty space into a full-fledged vintage furniture store. It looks as though it had always been there. Kyla's talents are on full display.

It's opening day. It all comes down to this. We rush to put together the last-minute details, neither of us expressing the pressure we feel. This has to succeed. The shadow of two years looms overhead. We bring it right down to the last minute with a surge of anxiety as we flip the sign in the door to "Open."

It's quiet. We watch people walk past the store, confused by what has magically appeared. All the hard work, all the uncertainty, my nerves are shot. And then it happens. The store comes alive. We're busier than our wildest dreams. By all metrics, it's a massive success.

The days are brutal, hitting estate sales in the early morning, keeping the store open until late in the evening. We set up the apartment in the back, collapsing on the air mattress every night. We immerse ourselves in the neighborhood, meeting other shopkeepers, eating lunch and dinner at the local spots. Just for this moment, this is our home and our community and I love it.

Before any of this happened, Kyla told me she wanted to move here. To this neighborhood. I resisted. I was afraid to leave the lifestyle of a town I could never achieve, the billionaires I was chasing. I was afraid of change.

I was worried I wouldn't fit in, afraid I would lose her to the neighborhood. I didn't fit in where we were living either, but there was security in what I knew. I'm beginning to see how much fear has cost me.

I think of my mom, her joy at working in the store, in being with us. I understand. This week is one of the most rewarding and fulfilling experiences of my life.

There's a flip side to the joy. I'm experiencing the torture of what could have been. If I had only listened to my heart and opened my eyes to what was always there.

TWELVE

*"One is never afraid of the unknown; one is
afraid of the known coming to an end."*
—JIDDU KRISHNAMURTI

WE KNEW THE DAY WOULD COME: *AUGUST 13, 2014,* WAS
tattooed on my brain. It doesn't make it any easier. The waiting
and planning are over. I'm going to prison.

I hold Matisse in my arms. I don't want to let go. I don't want
to let go of anything. She licks the tears off my face, no idea
what is happening, only that she is where she loves being, at
the center of the universe.

I look across our living room. Kyla is watching us with the
sadness of a thousand deaths. She may be witnessing the last
time I ever hold Matisse. The vet discovered a grapefruit-sized
tumor in her tiny body. We don't know how much longer we'll
have her. I find Athena and hold her, kissing her head. Typical
cat, she runs away at the first opportunity.

The moment is disrupted when the buzzer to our driveway gate rings. Looking at the camera, we see my dad and Paula have arrived. We only have another minute before we have to leave. I try to clean myself up, wiping the tears away. I take one last look at our home and Matisse, thinking to myself, *I will never see any of this again.*

We meet them on the sidewalk. Our hugs are filled with the weight of why they are here. Walking to Paula's car, I won't see any of this again either. Kyla and I sit in the back seat, Paula is driving, my father is navigating. I'm happy none of our neighbors is outside. I don't want to explain what today is.

The scenery becomes a blur. The trees, homes, and strip malls become one as we drive. The strip malls are replaced with pastures the further upstate we go. The rhythmic sound of the road provides background noise to our awkward conversation. With every mile, my life slowly vanishes. Federal prison is on the horizon.

I took swimming lessons when I was young. I hated it. Fear and anxiety would build with each passing day. On our way to the pool, I would count the rotations of the wheels. Each rotation brought me that much closer to what I was dreading. Here I am, once again, counting the rotation of the tires.

I haven't eaten since yesterday afternoon. Kyla pleaded with me to eat something, anything. With all the weight I'd lost, she was worried about my health.

"You have to eat something. You don't know when you will eat next."

All I can get down is half a banana. Even with all the pain I have caused, she's still trying to care for me. I'm not worthy of such love and care.

A sign appears in the distance: Otisville Federal Prison. We turn left onto One Mile Drive, carving our way up the mountain. My eardrums pop from the change in altitude. The road gives way to an open space, the prison coming into view.

Barbed wire fences marking the perimeter, the razor wire glistening in the sun. Guard towers looming high. Whatever air was in the car disappeared the moment we saw it.

Paula turns around and says, "You're not going in there."

I don't have much choice in the matter.

I say goodbye to my father and Paula in the parking lot.

"I'm so sorry. Thank you for everything. Please take care of her, protect her, whatever she needs. Please. Can you give her some money?"

They hold me tight and I say my final goodbye.

Kyla and I make the long walk across the parking lot and into the waiting room. I approach the security desk and check in.

The guard tells me, "Take a seat and wait. We'll call your name."

The room is cold, sanitary, and quiet. We sit side by side, holding each other's trembling hands. Looking into each other's eyes, I'm fighting the tears. I don't want to walk into prison a blubbering mess.

Our moment of silence is punctuated by the guard saying, "Stanland, Craig. It's time, say your goodbyes."

We kiss and hold each other. I'm afraid to let go. I fear what will happen when I do but I have to. I watch her walk out of prison as I walk in.

Both of us are walking into the unknown.

THIRTEEN

"If you want total security, go to prison. There you're fed, clothed, given medical care, and so on. The only thing lacking...is freedom."
–DWIGHT D. EISENHOWER

THE CO ESCORTS ME PAST THE SECURITY OFFICE, THE officers inside staring at me. His instructions come fast and forceful, "Shoes off, belt off, empty pockets, hands up, walk through the metal detector."

I rush to put my shoes and belt back on, grabbing the few things I brought with me. We walk a short distance to a set of double glass doors. The CO radios the security office.

"Prisoner move. Unlock A1."

Inquisitively, I look around for the inmate. It takes me a moment to understand it's me.

The security office unlocks the door, we walk outside. The twelve o'clock sun directly above, I squint as my eyes struggle to adjust. Cement sidewalks separated by patches of grass, a building in front of us. A double set of thirty-foot-high chain-link fences. If someone were to make it over one, they'd still have another to contend with.

Driving past prisons always sent a chill down my spine. They impose themselves on the landscape, casting a shadow on their surroundings—the barbed wire dividing them and us. The people on the other side of the fence are evil and dangerous. Prison is to be avoided at all costs.

Looking through the fence at the parking lot, the real world is only fifty feet away. So close, yet so far. It dawns on me: *I'm on the wrong side of the fence. I've become one of them.*

This is a little more real than I expected. My body is shutting down; autopilot is taking over. Pure survival mode.

Approaching the building in front of us, the CO once again radios the security desk. "Prisoner move. Unlock A2."

I don't look around this time.

We enter a long, windowless, colorless hallway. Bright fluorescent lights reflect off the white linoleum floors. Solid steel doors with exposed rivet heads every thirty feet.

Through one door, stop, wait for it to be unlocked. Walk through the door, stop, wait for it to be locked behind us. I lost count of how many we went through. I'm a ship traveling through the Panama Canal.

The only words spoken are "move" and "stop." The only sounds are our footsteps and the jingling of keys.

We walk into a large room. The CO informs me that we've arrived at our destination, R&D. Receiving and Departure. The four guards—three men and one woman—stare at me as we enter.

We approach a single holding cell. The battleship-gray bars are rough and chipped. Sliding a cartoonishly big skeleton key into the lock, a male guard swings open the door. He does not say a word. He doesn't have to. The moment I cross the threshold into the cell, the door slams behind me.

The sound of a door to a prison cell closing is the sound of freedom dying.

I look around. There isn't much to see. A wooden locker-room bench bolted to the cement floor, a stainless-steel toilet with a built-in sink, and nothing more. I pee and then sit down, resting my head in my hands. I know I have to pull it together. I need to stay in survival mode. I focus my attention on what I can hear and see. I'm searching for any piece of information that will make this process as smooth as possible.

A booming voice echoes through the hallway. Someone is on the wrong end of a verbal assault for being deceptive about their prescription med use.

"How can you tell me you do not take prescription drugs when you just told me you took a pill under a month ago? Do you even know what it means to take a pill? I'll give you one more chance to get your story straight."

I think to myself how stupid that guy is. *This isn't the place for lies. We're already caught. There's nothing more to get out of. We're in prison.* The guard who brought me here approaches my cell.

"Stanland. Medical. Let's go."

We walk a short distance to an examination room, sphygmomanometer on the wall, a scale in the corner, and a poster of the human anatomy hanging to my right. The guard leaves me alone with the woman sitting behind a small metal desk. She's middle-aged, slightly overweight, with short, blonde hair framing a cherubic face. She's so focused on the form in front of her, she doesn't acknowledge me.

After about a minute of silence, she puts her pen down, looks up, confirms my identity, and the procedure begins. She takes my blood pressure, higher than normal. Resting heart rate, higher than normal. Stepping on the scale, 109 pounds.

Otisville prison was built on a former tuberculosis sanatorium site. The original address was One Sanatorium Drive. Fittingly, she'd be administering a TB test. She explains the process.

"You'll be injected with a sterile solution containing tuberculin that will form a lump under your skin. You're to report back to the PA in three days. If the lump is still present, you have TB."

She carefully unpacks the syringe from its plastic pack and places it on the desk. As she reaches for a piece of paper, the needle rolls off the desk and onto the floor. We both stare as it bounces a few times before coming to rest under her chair.

Without uttering a word, she picks it up and places it back on the desk. She reaches for a bottle of rubbing alcohol and prepares the injection site at the crease of my arm.

How many people have walked on this floor? What was on the bottom of their shoes?

I'm trying to be respectful out of fear but I'm sure my panic is evident when I ask, "Are you going to get a new needle or clean that one since it fell on the floor?"

She picks her head up from what she's doing. A look of shock and confusion spreads over her face. Instantly I regret saying anything. She's pissed; her eyes squint in disdain.

She replies with a cold and deliberate, "No."

I understand what I am—a number, a body, and nothing more. I didn't dare speak as I watched the needle puncture my skin. I imagine diseases merging with my blood like cars on a highway.

Great, I'm going to be a convicted felon with HIV and Hep C.

She puts a Band-Aid on it like that's going to help. I feel like she's trapping the germs in my body.

Examination complete, the CO walks me to a small administrative office. Sitting behind the desk is the source of the booming voice. He's short, not much taller than me, salt-and-pepper hair. Cold, gray eyes and a severe face. He's holding my pre-sentencing report (PSR), a mini-biography of an inmate's life. I'm grateful I heard the first inmate go through this process. I know what to do. I know how to answer every question.

No extrapolating, no detailed descriptions. He has the PSR; he knows the answers to the questions he's asking. This is a test to see if I lie.

"When's the last time you've taken drugs?"

"Any psychological issues? Thoughts of suicide?"

"Are you on prescription medications?"

"Do you have any allergies I need to know about?"

"Are you fit to work?"

"Do you require a bottom bunk?"

"Are you religious?"

"Yes, sir," "No, sir," are all I say.

From the interview, I report to one of the guards. It's time for the strip search. We follow the same routine I did with the marshal, this time with full comprehension and no yelling. Standing naked, covering myself, freezing cold, and humiliated, the guard asks what size I wear.

Thinking it was fairly evident from my naked 109-pound frame, I reply, "Small."

I watch as he takes great pleasure in reaching for the shelf to the upper right, clearly marked "Extra Large." I would later learn this was the status quo, small guys get extra-large, big guys get extra-small. A joke the guards like to play on new inmates.

I'm issued my Federal Correctional Institution identification card. I'm inmate number 22052-014. I'm no longer the federal marshals' property. Now I belong to the Federal Bureau of Prisons.

Before coming here, I was given a list of items I could and could not bring. My vision is terrible. I rely on contact lenses to see. Contacts aren't allowed. Otisville does not want to be responsible for the additional medical care they believe contact lenses will entail. The prospect of wearing glasses for two years sucks. My prescription is old and the frame is weak.

I brought contact lenses with me, anyway, placing them inside my eyeglass case. Somehow thinking this was the ultimate hiding spot. Each guard who inspects my belongings yells the same thing.

"Stanland, what the fuck are these?"

"My contact lenses, sir."

"You can't have them. We'll throw them out."

"Yes, sir."

But no one threw them out. My contacts made it through every checkpoint, each guard threatening but none taking action. I'd like to think it was the kindness of the guards. In reality, I believe each one thought the other one was going to do it.

The receiving portion of the journey complete, it's time to go to my new home. Bedroll in hand, a guard brings me back through the labyrinth in which we came, all the way to the parking lot.

We are standing on the right side of the fence and I'm confused.

The guard points to a rock in the distance. "You see that rock? Walk to that rock and take a right—go up the hill. You'll see the camp and someone will meet you there."

Holding my pants up, I look at the guard towers looming overhead, thinking this was a trick, another joke the guards play on new inmates. I figured if I took one step, I was going to be shot.

The guard, used to this reaction, speaks with a grin. "Just stay on the path. You won't get shot."

Before surrendering, I was fortunate that I was counseled by a former inmate who set up a ministry to support white-collar criminals and their families.

Jeff told me what to expect, the rules of prison. How to behave. His help was immeasurable. He introduced me to another former inmate, Walt, who was also incredibly helpful. When the government informed me I was assigned to Otisville, Walt told me, "You hit the prison lottery."

When I make it up the hill, I understand.

There is no fence, the perimeter outlined by the edge of the woods. There are two single-story buildings, dull brown exterior, flat roofs, small windows. Picnic tables sit atop a hill of landscaped gravel and mulch, small plantings, and carefully placed boulders. All things considered, it actually looks nice.

There is an inmate on the sidewalk. He's enormous, six-foot-four, at least 260 pounds of what looks like pure muscle, bending at the waist petting a calico cat on the sidewalk. He's speaking lovingly to the animal. The cat trusts this man, rolling around, exposing her belly.

Seeing this moment of compassion gives me a sense that I'm going to be safe. My fears of physical assault vanished.

I've heard some inmates say their first night in prison is the best sleep they've had since the day of their arrest—the dark cloud, the anticipation, the unknown, all of it over. When I saw where I was and the people I would be living with, I knew I was safe. The fear of being raped, assaulted, all gone. It was not where I wanted to be, but the uncertainty I had feared for a year was over.

I fall right to sleep.

FOURTEEN

*"Your work is to discover your world and then
with all your heart give yourself to it."*
–BUDDHA

I'M ASSIGNED TO MY DORM. THERE ARE EIGHT BUNK BEDS,
two toilets, and one shower. I'm grateful there are several
windows. I was worried I'd be in the equivalent of a cave.

All sixteen beds were taken, so a temporary one was squeezed in
by the front door for me. Every time the door opens, it crashes
into my bed. I don't mind. It's an interesting way to meet people.

I like it in here. It's got a communal feel and everyone has been
incredibly kind.

Sal unofficially runs the dorm and his friend Pete assists. Pete
is as wide as he is tall, and I'm curious how he manages to
keep his silver hair styled so perfectly. I feel like I'm talking
to an extra from *Goodfellas* as he walks me through the dorm
rules.

"There are no locks on the bathroom doors, so you have to knock before you enter. No exceptions—you want to walk in on someone taking a dump? I didn't think so. Knock so they can hear you. No baby knocks. Let me hear you knock."

I give the door a good knock, hoping like hell there isn't anyone in there.

"Good. Good. Do that—every time. There's no toilet paper in the bathroom. You have to remember to bring your own. You have shower shoes? You don't want to take a shower without them. Ever. We turn the lights off at ten at night. Keep your area clean. Otherwise, they'll toss it."

"Toss it?"

Pete looks at me like I'm slow, "They'll throw all your shit on the floor, including your mattress."

I nod and say, "Oh."

It all seems very simple but I'm paying close attention. I don't want to screw anything up.

Sal has taken a liking to me and the feeling is mutual. He's funny and keeps the mood in the dorm light. He's been here a few years and knows what all the newbies are feeling.

I'm happy he likes me. He's the last person I would want to be at odds with. He's got to be at least six-four and 275 pounds. Most of it is muscle. It hurts my neck to look up at him when we speak. I'd later find out that the gigantic man I saw petting the cat is his brother.

I'm grateful for Sal and Pete. They invite me to their table for meals and introduce me to their friends.

When I'm not with them, I'm watching and observing the people who don't get harassed by the COs and the people who do. It's a lesson on how to behave and how not to behave. It comes down to being as conscientious as possible. To continually be aware of your surroundings and what time of day it is.

We're counted throughout the day to make sure we're all here and everyone keeps telling me, "Don't fuck up the count."

There are two counts during the week: 4 p.m. and 10 p.m. The weekends are confusing since they add a third at 10 a.m. We're required to stand for these counts. They also count us in our sleep, which I'm not as worried about.

The prison has obvious rules: no fighting, no weapons, no cell phones. But it's the unwritten inmate rules that are trickier.

Don't walk on a floor that an inmate just mopped.

Don't sit in any seat in the TV room without asking.

Don't be seen talking to the COs for too long. You don't want people to think you're a rat.

I don't know what the punishment would be for any of these infractions and I don't plan on finding out.

* * *

I've only been here a short while, but I'm settling in, finding a routine. Sal told me early on, "Prison is about beating the clock and a routine is how it's done. Find your routine."

I'm able to work out, which is awesome. The gym is in a steel Quonset hut with no heat or air conditioning, but it's got just enough equipment to get a good workout in. I read. Our library has over 7,000 books, I'm told.

Sal told the other inmates I used to be a personal trainer. I already have a full roster of clients to train.

I spend as much time outside as possible before the bad weather I keep hearing about forces us inside. Everyone, especially Pete, seems to enjoy telling me, "Don't get used to this. October is never this warm. Your skinny frame is never going to make it through these winters."

Great.

My prison friends have given me a prison nickname. I've had a smile on my face for as long as I can remember. It didn't take long for the others to notice.

I'm now "Smiley."

I was given a choice of work detail: the kitchen or the sewer plant. I chose the kitchen. So far, it's been the right call. Kitchen duty is the only job here that entails physical work, but we have access to extra food. Food, I am learning, is gold. I earn twelve cents an hour. If I keep up the good work, I will get a raise. Eighteen cents an hour. Fingers crossed.

I'm sitting at one of the picnic tables, happy to be alone. Solitude, I'm learning, is also gold. We're 118 guys confined to this space. Everyone makes it their business to know everyone else's business.

The shadows from the branches above are swaying back and forth across my pen and paper. I want to write what I'm feeling, to make sense of why I'm here, to release some of the pressure I feel building inside. It's not working. I know why I'm here. I just don't want to say it.

I put the pen down and take a moment to look around. I understand how fortunate I am, the relative beauty of this place. I did win the prison lottery. I'm not sure how well I would have coped serving time anywhere else.

It's the middle of the afternoon, my fellow inmates are engaged in their own routine, doing their own time. The gym is busy, rap music thumping. A couple of guys are playing handball. As I watch them play, I realize it's just paddleball minus the paddle. I don't know why I thought it was more complicated than that. I'm going to learn how to play but only with my left hand, just another thing to occupy my mind and distract me from what I've done.

I'm so far from where I want to be, yet I'm grateful to be where I am. That I'm safe. Feeling a sense of relief, my fears of being assaulted are gone. I see that this may be an opportunity, for what I'm not sure, but an opportunity, nonetheless. My mind relaxes. A sensation of pure, bright, brilliant light fills me from my core. It washes over me with the force of a tidal wave.

It feels as though I am connected to the universe and it's injecting the information directly into my brain. I feel energized and alive. I'm light enough to fly. This is one of the most beautiful sensations I've ever known. This is how I want to live my life.

I feel free, unburdened. I can take on the world and live an extraordinary life, all with what I feel inside. All the external, all the crap that I was chasing, none of it matters. Job titles, things, the constant comparison and racing with people I would never catch up to.

This is a moment in life—we only get a handful—that changes everything. I know as I feel the light wash over me, this will be something I'll never forget. Right now, right this moment, I want to live the hell out of this life and be free. I want to call Kyla, my family, and friends. I want to scream to the universe, *I get it! I see it now. I understand. Thank you, thank you, thank you. Please, can I try again? I won't fuck it up this time. Please let me have another chance.*

I have never wanted to live and experience life as much as I do at this moment.

Somebody yells something from the gym and I am yanked back to earth. I once again hear the rap music, the thud of a handball striking the wooden wall. I'm locked in prison and I put myself here. I can't go out and live life. I can't call anyone. I can't do a fucking thing and it's my fault.

I can't do anything with the gift I've been given. I can't go out and live life. I lost the freedom to do so. The world I want to experience isn't available to me.

A fist closes around my heart, choking the light out of me. I had it, I had it all, I always did. It was all inside of me and in front of me. And I threw it all away.

Only seconds ago, I was experiencing one of the most beautiful moments of my life. Now my world is shrinking.

I stare past the parking lot, down the hill to the edge of the woods, knowing that freedom is just on the other side. I'm trapped, alone with the man who took it all away and the knowledge.

"I've been given the secret to life and I'm helpless to do anything with it. This gift will die inside of me."

FIFTEEN

"Love never dies a natural death. It dies because we don't know how to replenish its source. It dies of blindness and errors and betrayals. It dies of illness and wounds; it dies of weariness, of witherings, of tarnishings."

—ANAÏS NIN

I PACE BETWEEN THE BUILDINGS LOOKING BACK AND forth at my watch and the driveway. Kyla's coming for a visit. I've never been this nervous about someone coming to see me. I feel something in the air. My friends keep telling me I'm overthinking. It's just a visit, nothing more. But I feel it. There was something in her voice. She knows something I don't. The sword of Damocles is hanging above my head. My heart falls into my stomach as our car comes around the bend.

She parks and makes the long walk up the hill. Hands buried in her coat pocket, her hair gently blowing in the wind. The weight of this place and life on her shoulders. She looks beautiful. She always does. Every day I would tell her she was the most beautiful woman in the world. And every day, my conviction in that statement grew stronger.

It's only three days before Christmas, so the visiting room is crowded. Barely a seat to be found, we squeeze into the crowd. The guard's desk, elevated on a platform, only a few feet away—an unwelcome reminder casting a shadow on the day. Not the environment either of us wants. None of this is.

The sound of a hundred conversations and a sea of green prison uniforms engulfs us. It's been just over four months. This surreal setting is now my home, in a world that is now my life. Her life is on the outside. Both under the same sun, moon, and stars but separated by so much more than prison walls.

I see something in her eyes, in the way she is sitting. There is something inside of her she wants to let out but is afraid to. But she has to. She doesn't want to keep it in. Maybe I'm manufacturing all of this, I don't know, but the conversation is forced and awkward. I just keep pushing. I know something is in there and I won't stop until I find it. Finally, I push hard enough.

With tear-filled eyes, she looks at me and says, "I'm leaving you."

I got what I was digging for and the sword came crashing down. Whatever piece of the outside world I had held onto, and I held it so tightly, so tightly I may have suffocated it, had vanished. My heart cried. I didn't mourn what I lost but the pain I had caused. Her pain was visceral; I felt it as if it were my own. And I'm responsible.

As much as I beg and plead with God—or whoever it is I'm begging to—I can't take away the betrayal. I can't take away the memory of opening the door to fifteen guns pointed at her face. I can't take away the invasion of our home, our beautiful home that she lovingly created. Every drawer, every facet of our life, opened and searched. I had destroyed our sanctuary.

I can't take back the lies. I destroyed the fundamental and beautiful foundation of a relationship. Trust in a relationship is a delicate dance. We share more of ourselves with every passing day. Taking the mask off and being seen and being loved as who we are. Years of building something beautiful, overturned in an instant.

I can't take away the fear, the uncertainty my choices created. The weight of her new business, the one she had dreamed of building, now tainted by the pressure of its success.

Her life is fourteen-hour days, returning home only to cook ground turkey for her and Matisse. She stands in the kitchen, eating it directly out of the pan. Then she fights to fall asleep, her mind racing about what didn't get done and what needs to be done. The work almost broke the two of us. I don't know how one person could actually do it on their own.

The first time I saw her, I was sitting at a bar, eating a burger, and drinking a Corona. She was waiting tables, waiting for the bartender to deliver her drink order. There was a light that radiated from her, filling every room she walked into. Her light was so bright, people talked about it when she wasn't even present. They'd say, "She has something about her…"

Now in this place neither of us want to be, I stare into her tear-filled eyes. The light is gone. In its place, fear, pain, sadness, betrayal, and anxiety.

Reaching my hand out to her long, graceful neck, she rests her head in my hand, giving herself over to a place of love and trust. Gently I squeeze and, without speaking a word, so much was said. This was another of our rituals. We would do this every day, throughout the day.

I leaned in and placed my lips on hers. In the middle of this chaos, we kissed. A kiss that both of us, in our hearts, knew was goodbye. A kiss of passion, love, regret, and sadness. Our tears coming together on our cheeks.

In between kisses, we talk. She looks at me, her cheeks shiny from tears. "What will you do for work?"

Great question and one I have been avoiding. I cannot go back to my old career. There is a court order barring me from working in that field. I am scared and don't know what I can do. I haven't thought about it yet. I'm still figuring out prison. My mind is searching for something, anything. *What will I do now? I have no future. How can I make money? How will I survive?*

I thought of her growing business, of the pop-up shop and how incredible an experience it was. How fulfilled I felt.

"Maybe I'll sell vintage furniture. I learned all I need to know from you, where to buy, how to sell, how to make things look good, and tie them together."

Her eyes come alive with anger. This would be another betrayal among many. Of all the jobs in the world, I chose the one option that puts us in direct competition with each other. I threatened the very thing she's barely holding together. The thing she's staked her survival on. I missed an opportunity to connect, to be honest, to say what was in my heart: *I'm scared. Please don't leave me. I understand what's important in life and I want to experience it with you.*

I didn't say any of that and I wouldn't have a chance to. Visiting time is over. She has to go. So much was said, so much left unsaid.

We kiss our last kiss and she walks out the door.

SIXTEEN

"Remorse is the poison of life."
−CHARLOTTE BRONTË

THERE'S A SADNESS IN THE AIR. IT'S NOT JUST MINE; IT belongs to all of us. None of us complains. What's the point? We're all in the same boat, all wishing we weren't. We keep our wishes to ourselves, doing our best to maintain our routines, all the while struggling with what we should be doing, not what our reality is. There's no reason to say it because we're all thinking the same exact thing.

We all wish we were home with our families doing whatever each of us does on Christmas Day. There is a collective, unspoken desire that Christmas disappears just for the time we are in prison. We'd like to skip the day or at least be unaware of it.

I should be home but I'm not. I should be waking up next to her, kissing her shoulder, wishing her a Merry Christmas, as she rolls over with a sleepy smile, saying, "Hi, baby, Merry Christmas."

I can hear her morning voice in my ear, not yet awake, soft and gentle. I love it.

I should be bringing her lavender tea in bed and the first present of the day. I should be next to her, celebrating not only Christmas but the anniversary of my proposal. We should be sitting on the floor, under the light of the tree, opening our presents, opening Matisse's and Athena's gifts. We should be making breakfast.

We should be together. But we're not and it's my fault. I want to escape the regret and the weight of this day. I look to our last Christmas together but I ruined that one too. We woke to the shadow of prison in the air and the pain from the accident in our bones. Two Christmases have been destroyed and I'll be here for the next one as well.

This isn't Christmas. It isn't an anniversary. It's just another day I want to end.

SEVENTEEN

"Shame is a soul-eating emotion."
—C.G. JUNG

I'M AWAKE, BUT I DON'T WANT TO OPEN MY EYES. I'M
afraid to let reality in. I don't need the reminder—my mind
is prison enough. I can't handle it yet. I know what's waiting
for me, the same thing every morning—concrete cubicles and
inmates. I listen as people start their day, the sound of shower
shoes clip-clopping down the hallway, running water from the
showers, toilets flushing: the tap, tap, tap of a disposable razor
against the sink.

I know when I open my eyes, the world will expand. My emptiness will explode.

She's leaving me. The pain in her voice runs through my veins.
I see the hurt and love in her eyes on the back of my eyelids.
I destroyed the greatest thing I've ever experienced in my life.
Truth is, I killed it a long time ago. It just took this long to die.

I did this and I fucking hate myself for it.

I hate the choices I made. I hate who I've become. I hate how I lived. I hate that I betrayed myself. I hate the lies I told. I hate that I don't trust myself. I hate that I was so fucking ignorant and arrogant. I hate that I am afraid to open my eyes. I hate that I live inside this body with the man who's responsible. It's been a year of wanting to rip my skin off, a year trapped with myself. It's exhausting.

I want a new body. I want new memories.

I have twenty months left. Twenty months to remember that she won't be there when I get out. Twenty months of living with the consequences. Twenty months of opening my eyes to concrete cubicles and inmates. My existence is a permanent reminder of how much I hate myself.

I need to lie here a little longer, to let the pain in. I want it to consume me. I want to drown in it. It's what I deserve.

I had love and I destroyed it. The greatest gift that life can give and I sacrificed it. The universe, my heart, my friends, my family, and my wife all tried to guide me differently and I ignored them all. Out of fear.

What was I so afraid of? Why did I sacrifice so much for so little?

Why?

I think about my family, how I haven't told them yet. What will I say to them? They'll be sad and hurt. They don't want to lose her but they'll understand why she must go. They will support me and I'm scared of it. Every act of kindness—every bit of love—burns. It burns like my heart is pumping rubbing alcohol. There is no escape from it.

I know I can't stay in bed forever. I know I have to open my eyes—concrete cubicles and inmates. The world expands, my emptiness explodes.

The emptiness is replaced with reality. *What do I have to do today? It's Tuesday and I have to work. Burgers for lunch and pizza for dinner. What sides are we making with each meal? Has the cheese for the pizza been delivered yet? I hope the burgers aren't frozen together like last time. How much food can I steal to give to my friends?*

I'm somewhere other than my mind and it's nice. I don't deserve nice. I'm not worthy of it. I'm not worthy of the distractions reality is providing.

I let the pain back in. I let the emptiness run wild. It has to occupy the same space as reality. It's what I deserve for what I've done.

EIGHTEEN

"Everyone who wills can hear the inner
voice. It is within everyone."
—MAHATMA GANDHI

THE VOICE WAS THERE. IT WAS ALWAYS THERE. IT DID what it was meant to do and it worked diligently to fulfill its purpose. The voice is what's missing. This is why I feel empty.

Spoken from the heart, it's the sincerest form of communication I've ever known. The voice is the unconditional love for ourselves that lives within us. It's our guide. It speaks in words. It speaks in emotions. It manifests itself physically. A fist clenched around my heart, a sinking feeling in the pit of my stomach.

My voice spoke every language at its disposal and I ignored them all. I ignored it for too long and too often, so it left. It's the foundation of self-trust: no foundation, no trust.

The voice filled me up. I'm empty without it. My chest has the density of a black hole with the infinite pull of shame and regret. The pain is excruciating. I don't know how to fix it. This isn't like a cut or a bruise. There are no Band-Aids or icepacks that will make it go away.

I miss my voice. I miss my guide. I'm lost without it and don't trust myself to know how to get it back.

I knew better. And knowing that is torture.

NINETEEN

"*I cannot shake the image that 2015 is going to be the year I put a bullet in my head. I see myself making it through prison, making it to halfway. The next vision I see is a pistol w/a silencer in my mouth or at my temple. I want to tell someone but I'm ashamed. I'm ashamed of being weak. I know how much it would hurt my loved ones. But the way I feel, the self-loathing, the amount of shame I carry, I have a hard time being in front of my loved ones. I'm no good to them. I can't even face them. Why won't it just end?*"
—JOURNAL ENTRY, JANUARY 1, 2015

TWENTY

*"The thought of suicide is a great consolation: by
means of it, one gets through many a dark night."*
–FRIEDRICH NIETZSCHE

FOR THE PAST SEVERAL YEARS, I'VE WANTED TO LEARN
how to meditate. I thought it would give me an edge at work,
that it would make me better than my peers. When I read blog
posts on peak performance, meditation is always on the top of
the list. I'd say to myself, "Yeah, I should do that…"

I never did. I always had an excuse, not enough time. *I'll start
tomorrow. How can I get the effects without doing the work? Is
there a shortcut?* Always looking for the easy way.

I don't have excuses anymore and I need something to help pass
the time. I've been practicing. There are a few meditation books
in the library and my family has sent some as well.

I focus, at least try to, on my breath or mantra when I meditate.
My mind wanders, away from the breath, away from the mantra.
The same thing that happens to everyone who meditates. My

monkey mind runs the projector in my brain, presenting pictures and thoughts, one after another, until one of them seizes my attention.

It's absurd what my mind comes up with. From Kyla to losing everything, my car, my Facebook page, Athena, what is this person saying about me? Who is happy that this happened to me? Will the restaurants we frequented wonder what happened to us? Will I ever own a house again? I obsess over my credit score. I haven't paid any credit card bills in months.

The monkey is a hard worker, inserting slide after slide into the projector, looking for the one thought or image that will stick. A few days after Kyla's visit, just after Christmas, the monkey found it. It's not an image. It's a short film.

I'm looking at a cold, dark, dingy basement, the cinder block walls repainted countless times throughout the years. Hints of green, orange, and yellow revealing themselves through the chipped paint.

There is a small window; the glass is warped and blackened by years of filth and neglect. The window frame is splintered and rotting. The wood is old and gray. I don't know what time of day it is. The only light in the room is coming from a single low-watt bulb hanging from the rafters. It's cockeyed. One wire is cut shorter than the other.

A wooden chair sits to the left of the window, facing away from the wall. One of its legs hovers an inch above the floor. The layer of dust tells the story of a time gone by.

A man enters the room. Even with the black hood over his face,

I know it's me. I feel his hopelessness in my heart. I sit on the chair as it wobbles back and forth.

Suddenly, I reach under the chair and pull out a pistol. I don't know where it's hidden, only that it's there. I put the gun in my mouth. I can taste the cloth and feel the cold steel of the barrel. I don't wait long to pull the trigger. Chunks of brain and skull stick to the wall, slowly moving down as gravity takes over. The chair wobbles, my body slumps forward.

The monkey projected this short film over and over. It wouldn't stop.

Rewind; hit play.

Rewind; hit play.

Rewind; hit play.

Drops of water eventually create a canyon. This perpetual loop carves itself into my brain. The sensations become real. My feet on the cement floor, my butt on the chair, the tension of the trigger testing my finger. I feel the bullet entering and exiting my skull. After four months of living with this scene every second of every day, I'm losing my fucking mind.

I want it to end. I need it to stop.

My resources are limited, but there are a couple of options. I could hang myself in the gym. I keep thinking Sal would be the one to find me: my lifeless body, hanging from the pull-up bar. I can't do that to him after all he's done for me. He's been an amazing friend, all the while contending with his own problems, his own heartbreak. Caught up in some crap his brother was doing, he has four years left. I can't do that to him.

Another option is hanging myself in the woods, but spring hasn't started. There are no leaves to hide behind. If I'm caught entering the woods, I'll be charged with escape. An immediate two more years added onto my sentence in a facility that's not a camp. The threat of even more time, having to worry about my physical safety. This isn't an option.

I think of Kyla and the pain it would cause. I would be responsible for creating even more hurt. Just one more selfish act on top of the selfishness that put us in this position.

I can't find the courage or creativity to move past these obstacles.

I'm a worthless coward who can't figure out how to kill himself.

I spend my days trapped in the movie of blowing my brains out, wishing it would stop, and waiting for the ten o'clock count so I can go to sleep. Sleep makes it stop, if only temporarily.

I follow the same routine every night. Sitting in my bunk, reading, waiting for the CO on duty to yell, "Count!" Climb out of the bunk, wait to be counted, climb back into bed, and wait for sleep.

As much as I look forward to this moment, another day done, it's also the worst part of my day. These few minutes scare the hell out of me.

The accumulation of shame, the vision of blowing my brains out, feeling like a worthless coward, and mistrust reaches a crescendo in the moments before sleep overtakes me. I'll never be whole. I'll always be empty. I want to cry, to scream, to be free from this. You don't cry in prison. I do not want to be that guy.

Instead, I beg and plead for it to stop—for the torture of being trapped in my body with this mind to just stop. If I die from natural causes, I could get what I want and not hurt anyone. The movie would stop playing. I pray to God or anyone else who will listen to kill me in my sleep. I'm not asking for much, just stop my heart, take my breath. I beg Death to do me this favor, the same prayer every night.

Why won't it stop? Why won't it stop? Why won't it stop? Please make it fucking stop…Please make it fucking stop…

Eventually, through utter exhaustion, sleep comes. I'm granted an eight-hour reprieve.

Every morning I'm disappointed when my eyes open to the light of a new day. My prayers have gone unanswered for four months. The monkey is on the same schedule I am. I wake up, he wakes up. He goes right back to work, pressing play, and the day begins.

I live up to my nickname, smiling and pretending everything is okay. I'm afraid to share the thoughts I'm having with anyone.

The rumors around being suicidal in prison scare the hell out of me. Supposedly they take everything away from you and lock you in solitary. You stay there until you are no longer a threat to yourself or others, only to be shipped to a mental facility.

I need someone to talk to, to share what is really going on in my mind, behind the smile. I can't share with my friends. I worry they'll tell a guard or the camp counselor. Not to be malicious but because they care about me. I can't mention it on the phone or in an email; everything is monitored.

I meet with the prison psychologist, delicately explaining my situation, the threat of solitary hanging over my head.

My wife is leaving me. I lost everything...I don't know what to do.

She wears her disinterest on her sleeve. She abruptly ends the session by handing me a single sheet of paper, "What to Do If You're Depressed," a ten-step generic guide, containing such gems as: "exercise," "start a hobby," and "talk to a friend."

Meeting with her makes me feel even worse. I'm embarrassed I shared anything at all. I can't imagine the horrors she witnesses at the medium-security prison. Who am I to whine?

My life has no purpose other than passing the time. Routine and death are my companions. Routine dictates I check email at two o'clock in the afternoon. We're fortunate to have email, even if the system is primitive. No spellcheck, no pictures, and no attachments allowed, but it gets the job done.

Logging on, I see one new message from Sean, my best friend of over thirty years. He was the other best man at my wedding. We went to the same schools since kindergarten and became friends in the ninth grade when his family moved and we found ourselves on the same bus. Sean was the first person I called after I was sentenced.

It was a simple, to-the-point email: "Hey man, can I come for a visit this weekend?"

I stare at the email. Not too many people ask to come to prison. I feel torn, equal parts of excitement and stress.

Receiving a visit in prison is as stressful as it is incredible. We're thrilled to see a different face, to have a connection to the outside world but stressed to face the shame, guilt, and embarrassment of a loved one seeing us in this place.

Visits make me feel like an animal in a zoo. Like I'm on exhibition. And in a sense, rightfully so. Inmates are the anomaly of society. Almost all the people who come to visit me comment about scratching a prison visit off their bucket list. Prisoners have the stories to tell, the situations and circumstances that can only occur in prison. Visits remind me of what I did and what I lost.

I was prepared to be the animal in the zoo, my stories set. I want to share with him the thoughts I'm having. To tell him how I pray for death every night. I need this outlet and I need it now.

I watch him park his white Dodge Ram pickup truck and make the same walk Kyla made up the hill into the visiting room. It's been just over a year since I've seen him. He looks tired.

We find some open seats a little away from the crowd. The green vinyl creaks like an old car seat as we settle in. Sean purchases food from the vending machine. He has to buy it himself; I'm not allowed to touch money. We both dig into some micro-waved cheeseburgers and root beer, a much-needed break from prison food. I wonder if I've aged as much as he has in this past year.

The Metallica song "Nothing Else Matters" speaks of trust and where we find it.

In the twenty-seven years since the album's release, I can't remember a time hearing James Hetfield sing that song that I haven't thought of Sean. I can trust him. I can let it out.

The pressure is building inside of me. I need to let the words out. I need to get these demons out of me. I feel the anticipation, the excitement, the relief. I open my mouth to speak, to free myself from this hell, but I can't find the words.

Before I utter a word, Sean leans forward in his seat and opens up. The words pour out of him. He's releasing his own demons. His life is a mess, divorce and money issues, sadness, and hurt.

The pain he's experiencing is written in his eyes, his voice. My best friend is suffering. He came to see me—not only to be my friend but because he needed his friend. He needed an outlet and he chose me.

When Sean came to visit me in prison, he did not see what I do when I look in the mirror. He saw his friend. I was not my things. I was not my job. I was not what I could buy. I was not the horrible person who destroyed lives.

I was a friend he trusted with the pain he was experiencing.

Four months of watching myself blow my brains out, four months of living in pure hell came to a screeching halt. I'm not worthless. I'm not empty. I'm not the things I own. Sitting in a prison visiting room with nothing to my name, I feel more whole than I've felt in years.

I don't know if he understands the magnitude of what just happened inside of me. My heart speaks. My voice is back.

I am not empty. I am not alone.

We speak for a while about his life and I watch as the burden he was carrying slowly drops from his broad shoulders. I don't need to tell him everything I've been experiencing. I need to listen. As I do, I wonder if he sees the burden that I've been carrying fade away as well.

Once we get the serious stuff out of the way, we settle in. He tells me what Jason, Rob, and Chris are up to. I tell him the ridiculous stories that can only happen in prison. We laugh like the lifelong friends we are. His laugh lines have grown. I'm sure mine have too.

Eventually, it's time for him to go home. I walk with him as far as I'm allowed. We hug each other tightly, each with respect for the bond we share. He walks out the door. I'm sad to see him leave, yet grateful that I already miss him.

The following week my mom and aunt come to visit. They heard the pain and suffering in my voice. They read it in the emails we exchanged. My mom flew up from North Carolina and together they drove from my aunt's home in Connecticut. Otisville is located near Woodbury Commons, an outlet center for designer labels. They were combining a prison visit and a shopping spree. How many people can make that claim?

My mom sets the tone for our visit as she looks around the room, the way people look around when they're about to do something or say something they're not supposed to do or say. The coast is clear. She slowly reaches into her bag, pulling out a napkin wrapped around something. She places it in the middle of the table and the three of us stare at it like it's going to perform a trick. I have no idea what's going on. With the biggest smile, she unwraps the napkin, exposing what is inside. She "stole" free cookies from the hotel lobby and smuggled them into prison.

We share a bonding moment between criminals. They're the best cookies I've ever had: chocolate chocolate chip, soft in the middle, with crispy edges, perfect. Their love, their support, following their intuition, all of it radiating through, all of it filling me up.

A few mornings after the visits, I'm different. I wake up in a way I haven't experienced in four months—something's missing. There's no disappointment seeing the light of a new day.

I wake up experiencing the peace of knowing I'm not empty. The peace of knowing I have worth.

TWENTY-ONE

*"Every second, a seeker can start over, for his life's
mistakes are initial drafts and not the final version."*
−SRI CHINMOY

THE EDUCATION BUILDING IS QUIET. ED AND I ARE THE
only inmates walking down the hallway. The freshly mopped
floor reflects the fluorescent lights above. The camp counselor is
in his office, behind a wall of glass, staring at a computer monitor. The whiteboard behind him is marked with new arrivals
and pending releases. The new arrivals are in red, the pending
releases in blue. Another four months or so and my name will
be in blue.

Ed walks with slightly rounded shoulders; his belly, the product of an Oreo addiction, pulls them forward. With silver hair,
glasses, and wisdom in his eyes, he manages to look distin-
guished even in prison greens.

Not only was Ed my mentor when I first arrived but we also
share a love of Oreos. If anyone ever ran out, they knew Ed
and I were the people to go to. I'm grateful he chose to mentor

me; he knows the ins and outs of this place and has a calming demeanor.

We're talking about what I'm going to do and what plans I have. I'm sharing my fears about life on the outside, the unknown future. Who I was no longer exists. What will I do with my life? There is a court order barring me from my past profession. Who would hire an ex-con? My wife is divorcing me, reinforcing the belief I will fail in all future relationships. I question who would date an ex-con anyway. I have no home. The idea of facing life without love and connection, without the security of a paycheck and a place to call home, is devastating. Prison may be horrible but it is a bed and three meals a day.

With his hands in his prison greens, Ed listens, having heard similar concerns from the inmates who passed through his life. A former hedge fund manager, he was found guilty of committing wire fraud to the tune of $60 million. He's only five years into a nine-year sentence. He keeps himself busy mentoring new inmates, running the education department, and perhaps most importantly, coordinating the TV programming every night. He's got a gift for it. We watch great movies and he always gets us out before the ten o'clock count.

We pause at the entrance of the education room. We're early for the anger management class. He's teaching and I'm a student. I don't have anger issues but prison is like high school. Certain courses look good on your transcript. Plus, it helps pass the time and Ed keeps it interesting by bringing up issues in the camp: who's got a beef with whom. He takes his hand out of his pocket and places his arm around my shoulder. It's nice to feel human contact.

Ed looks me in the eyes and a slight smile appears on his face as he confidently pronounces, "Craig, you have a blank canvas. Paint whatever picture you want."

TWENTY-TWO

*"Faith is taking the first step, even when
you don't see the whole staircase."*
−MARTIN LUTHER KING JR.

"YOU HAVE A BLANK CANVAS. PAINT ANY PICTURE YOU want."

Great. How?

When Ed said those words in the hallway, they were inspiring and empowering. They were just what I needed until reality kicked in. I have no clue what I want. I have no idea who I want to be or what I want to be. I don't know what picture to paint. I don't even know how to paint.

During a session with my pre-prison counselor, Jeff, he told me about a stockbroker arrested for insider trading. He lost everything and had a sentence a little longer than mine. He had a blank canvas too.

After prison, he moved to the Caribbean to teach tourists how to windsurf. He's never looked back and has never been happier. Perfect. I love the beach. I love the Caribbean.

I found the picture I want to paint. Oh, wait. I can't swim more than thirty feet without getting winded and I panic when my feet don't touch the bottom. And I've never windsurfed.

Painting whatever picture I want is turning out to be both incredibly inspirational and seemingly impossible. This once-in-a-lifetime opportunity to start over is turning into paralyzing fear. How do I rebuild my life when I'm the one who destroyed it? I have to rely on myself, the guy who fucked it all up, to put it back together? I'm consumed by fear, uncertainty, regret, anxiety, the torture of self-mistrust.

None of this seems to be an optimal starting point.

Alone in my cube, feeling completely lost and confused, something dawns on me. Taking inventory, there is one thing I have in abundance.

Time.

I can choose to make the remainder of my sentence a gift or I can squander it. The responsibilities of the outside world, the real world, are on the back burner for now. Bills, work, taxes, divorce: I can't do anything about these things in prison. My environment is safe. I have food and shelter.

I have nothing to worry about other than trying to put my life back together.

I need some quiet time to figure this out. I grab my journal and a pen and head to the library. Fortunately, it's empty. I sit in my usual spot in the back and to the right. Opening the journal, pen in hand, the gift of time has not reduced the task's immensity.

As I stare at the blank page, analysis paralysis fully kicks in. I can't envision a future that's colored by the arrest, prison, and suffering. I don't know how I'll experience joy or happiness. I don't know how to trust myself.

With no idea how to move forward, my instinct tells me to go backward. *Why did I ignore the obvious? Why did I make the choices I made? What was missing? What was I trying to fill? Why did I sacrifice so much for so little?*

The questions sting. My gut tells me this means I'm on the right track. I've never asked myself questions like these. I didn't have to. I was fine the way I was. My belief was, I'm smart. Nothing else needs to be done. The irony that my "smarts" are a part of what landed me in prison sits squarely on my shoulders.

The questions are too complicated. They sting too much. I'm ready to give up painting whatever picture I want before I even pick up a brush. I'm going to squander my opportunity. The canvas will remain blank.

Out of sheer frustration, I throw the pen down and mutter, "Okay, fine…what can I do?"

I stop in my tracks. I write it down.

"What can I do?"

These four words provide possibilities, not limits. Approaching a complex issue with a simple question levels the playing field.

The answer comes to me. It was simple and clear. It's a concept that's survived for thousands of years. I didn't understand the beauty and simplicity until I was presented with what seems to be an insurmountable obstacle. Lao Tzu said it perfectly: "The journey of a thousand miles begins with one step."

I'm not going to paint this picture in one sitting. What is the one brushstroke that will start this journey?

The door to the library opens. I don't look to see who it is. I'm hoping to remain hidden, wishing they would go away so I can rebuild in peace. I wish I didn't have to rebuild. I wish I had made a different choice. I wish I were home with Kyla, Matisse, and Athena. I wish I could change what cannot be changed. I'm in a fight I can never win.

I know what the first brushstroke must be.

TWENTY-THREE

*"God grant us the serenity to accept the things we
cannot change, the courage to change the things we
can, and the wisdom to know the difference."*
−REINHOLD NIEBUHR

I SPEND HALF OF MY TIME WISHING I WASN'T IN PRISON,
the other half wishing I had made a different choice. I fantasize
about going back in time to the day I discovered the loophole
I exploited. I see myself at the dining room table, staring at my
laptop. A black-and-white composition notebook to my right,
the pages filled with notes, yellow Post-its stuck everywhere. I
look like John Nash in *A Beautiful Mind.*

The puzzle pieces were coming together. I had discovered a
treasure map that only I knew about. I feel the excitement I
felt, the pure rush of it all. My performance at work was not
what it used to be; my paychecks were shrinking. My need to
buy more things, to fill the hole inside, was growing. This was
a lousy equation but I had solved it.

I wish I could travel back to that moment, to speak louder than the rush and say, "Stop. Don't do this. You have everything you need. This is not the way."

I would have made a different choice. The first domino would have never fallen, the criminal complaint never filed, the investigation never initiated. The FBI wouldn't have aimed fifteen guns at Kyla. I wouldn't have hurt the people I love. I wouldn't have to strip naked, lift my balls, spread my cheeks, and cough. I'd be free. The short film of my suicide would have never been produced.

The voice was there and I knew it. I chose to ignore it. In those moments of clarity, when I calculated the damage done, my heart tightened. I felt like I was always on the verge of a heart attack. I tried to erase the pain with lies, and it usually worked— at least for a little bit.

I wish I had listened to that voice. But I didn't. Now I'm sitting in a prison library trying to start over. I will never have the freedom to paint whatever I want if I continue to fight what can't be changed. I must do what I am afraid to do.

I have to practice acceptance.

I don't want to. It feels like giving up, passive. Fighting equals progress. But does it? What am I fighting against? As much as I wish it existed, there's no such thing as a DeLorean time machine.

I've locked myself in a past that can't be changed, in an existence that fills me with shame and regret. Fighting isn't progress; it's running away from the truth.

I was wrong: Acceptance isn't giving up, and it isn't passive. It is an act of courage to say, "I accept that I betrayed myself and chose to commit a crime." I hit the *Enter* button, the single keystroke that started it all. "I accept I made the choice to continue in the face of the universe screaming at me to stop. I accept that I'm in prison. I accept that I hurt the woman I love, my family, my friends. My finances are in ruin; I'm getting divorced. I'll have a criminal record until I die. I accept that I don't trust myself. I accept that I'm scared."

Holy crap, that felt good. I don't feel as trapped. I feel something extraordinary. I'm in prison but I just gave myself freedom. No one else, nothing external, I did this.

A thought pops into my head: *This is my life now. What am I going to do with what is left of it?*

TWENTY-FOUR

"The sun shines not on us but in us."

—JOHN MUIR

I STEP OUTSIDE, MY HANDS FULL OF BOOKS, JOURNALS, and a cup of coffee. It's a balancing act, one I've gotten pretty good at. The fall air feels good on my face, wakes me up. It's quiet. The birds aren't even awake.

The sun has not risen above the horizon and already its artistry has begun, the eastern sky ablaze in color. To the west, the light of a few lonely stars fade. I look at where yesterday meets today, the black of night transforming into the dawn of a new day. Black to blue to purple, a cool pink on the fringe.

The forest is alive with color, the fall foliage reflecting the morning light, oranges, reds, and yellows. The oak trees, always the last to turn, still holding their green leaves.

I breathe deeply, a moment of peace as I stand before nature's majesty. Exhaling, I see it's a little cooler than I thought. Every morning is a new display, a new piece of art. I've never experienced sunrises like this—like snowflakes. No two are the same, but equally stunning. I watch the scene unfold, forgetting where I am, lost in the ever-changing movie playing out across the sky. The medium-security prison, off in the distance, ceases to exist. If only for a second.

I may be in prison, but every clear morning I escape. The beauty of being connected to nature; it's bigger than this place. The magic of the world we live in when we stop and take the time to just be. My circumstance can't be changed and it's not what I want. But my interactions with it, what I do with what I have, that's mine.

Nature's exhibition doesn't end with the sunrise. The sunsets are equally as beautiful. The mornings are filled with darker, cooler, crisper colors. The evenings are on the warmer end of the color spectrum: pastel oranges, yellows, and pinks.

I understand why Monet preferred to paint by the morning and evening light. The colors are more alive. I'm humbled by the sheer size of nature, feeling very small and, oddly, very large at the same time. It's as though I am one with the world.

I think of Kyla. I wish I could share this with her. I can't. I lost that privilege. A wave of sadness washes over me. I find hope in the thought that wherever she is, she's seeing what I'm seeing and feeling what I'm feeling: just a little peace, a mini escape.

Walking into the education building, I settle into the library. For now, I'm the only one here. I sit in my usual spot. I treasure these moments of solitude.

Since hearing Ed's words, life is different after the visits from

Sean, my mom, and aunt. I'm a little more open to this experience. I'm reading more, having a bit more fun. The need to punish myself is still strong but I'm working on it. I'm assembling a morning routine, wondering how I can make something of my terrible choice.

I open my black marble composition notebook and take the cap off the pen. Placing the pen to paper, I write, "I am grateful for this morning's sunrise and that I was able to experience it."

That felt good. With just one sentence, the mind opens to other things I am grateful for:

"...my instant coffee, and the powdered cream tasted particularly good this morning. Yesterday's workout was really good. I'm grateful for feeding Beers. I'm grateful that he smiles when he waddles over to me. Can a goose smile? I'm grateful he's safe, even with the broken wing. Who named him Beers anyway? I'm grateful I have the library to myself for now."

I do this again tomorrow and the day after and the day after that. I don't miss a day. It's not easy finding things to be grateful for in prison. Maybe that's what makes the practice so powerful, because, no matter what, I always find something.

TWENTY-FIVE

"Comparison is the death of joy."
—MARK TWAIN

WHEN I ARRIVED AT OTISVILLE, I WAS ISSUED FOUR brown T-shirts, four green shirts, two pair of green pants, a pair of steel-toe boots, four pairs of socks, four pairs of boxers, one pillow, one sheet, one blanket, and a windbreaker jacket.

I purchased items from the commissary: gray sweats, T-shirts, boxer briefs, and thermals. I received free clothes, boots, and sneakers from soon-to-be-released inmates. It's a prison tradition: You give what you no longer need to those who do. I have notebooks and pens and books sent by family and friends.

I live in a concrete cubicle measuring approximately eight-by-twelve. An exercise in minimalism, it's filled with a bunk bed, a storage locker the size of an end table, five hooks to hang my clothes, and a plastic stool shaped like a mushroom.

The beds are narrow, about the size of a camping cot, covered with cheap vinyl mattresses that sag in the middle. No decorations or personalization are allowed. Purposeful, sanitary, and emotionless.

I share this space with my bunkie, Hassan. A multimillionaire in his mid-sixties. Hassan's sentence provides perspective for my own. He's only halfway through a twelve-year sentence for committing financial fraud.

A Harvard graduate, he's one of the smartest and wisest men I've ever met. We laugh, we bullshit, he listens to my relationship worries, he shares his wisdom and experience. When he's finished with whatever magazine or newspaper he's reading, he kicks the bottom of my bunk and hands it up to me. I'm grateful to have him as a bunkie.

I return to our cube after a workout. He's lying on his bunk, reading a book. He looks at me, marks his page, sets it down, and says, "Take a seat, give me a moment."

I sit on my plastic mushroom stool as he climbs out of his bunk and steps onto the floor. Stretching his arm under the bed, he reaches for the boxes he tucks out of view from the COs and the camp administrator.

With a little effort, he pulls a cardboard box from under the bed. Sorting through books, papers, and letters, he finds what he is looking for—a photo album. The leather is soft and supple, its ivory color a glaring juxtaposition to the coldness of this place. I stare at it, thinking, *That's the prettiest thing in this place.*

He opens to the first page, a beautiful bride in a flowing white dress, her eyes the epitome of joy. I feel a wave of sadness and loss when I realize what he's sharing with me.

He missed his daughter's wedding because of his choices. This photo album is all he has to connect him to that day. His son walked her down the aisle. It should have been him. His eyes fill with sadness and joy that can only be born from unconditional love.

He holds the album with reverence, turning the pages slowly and carefully. As he speaks, his hand gently runs over the images, his way of connecting to that day. He invites me on his mini escape, bringing me into each scene, telling me who these strangers staring back at me are and sharing all the details of the English countryside and the rustic castle. I don't care that I don't know any of these people and never will.

If only for a moment, Hassan and I are somewhere else.

Before being arrested, I would have compared myself to Hassan. His wealth, his education, his wisdom, his life experience. Measuring his things against my things, falling short, every time. Feeling less than enough, less than worthy. Desperately wanting to catch up, never understanding that there would never be enough to fill what was missing inside of me. Comparison shrunk my world.

Now, in our cube, surrounded by our meager possessions, none of that is important. Not our homes, cars, watches, dinners, or careers. Sitting side by side, there is no material possession, aside from this photo album, that matters. I'm not comparing or trying to match or beat him. We're enjoying a moment of shared sadness, joy, and humanity.

Things are external. Things are fleeting. What I'm experiencing right now flows from inside. It can't be lost or stolen without my consent.

TWENTY-SIX

*"There is no greater joy in life than the
joy of creating something."*
—ABHAY KUMAR

I GET TO THE KITCHEN EARLY. I'M HAPPY THE OTHER GUYS
have not shown up yet. I have an idea: to try something, to do
something for my friends. The stainless-steel table is set and
I'm ready to begin.

I've got a box of oranges, the green plastic cutting board, a huge
steel bowl, and a knife tethered to the table to prevent us from
stealing it or killing one another. I have everything I need.

One by one, I cut the oranges in half, placing them on the cutting board. Perfectly lined up, five rows of eight. Starting at the
top left, I take the first half in my hand, squeezing with all my
might. The juice sprays everywhere, running over my fingers,
eventually reaching the bowl. The smell of citrus overwhelms
the stagnation of the kitchen.

The industrial prison fridge is colder than my refrigerator at home. My hand is numb after the tenth squeeze. I alternate from right to left until the last of the juice has been extracted.

Our utensils and tools in the kitchen are limited. I do my best to spoon the seeds out. It seems impossible to get them all. I've never seen so many seeds. I blame the cheap prison oranges. Placing a row of plastic cups on the table, I carefully fill them all with the precious juice. I crouch down, eyeballing the amount in each glass, ensuring everyone gets an equal share, and transferring from one cup to another until all are even.

I'm not supposed to be doing this. Freshly squeezed orange juice is not on the menu and therefore should not be made. Technically, I'm breaking a rule. I don't care. This is something I wanted to do—for myself and my friends.

I like the work, the process, focusing on a task. The creation of something from scratch, even if it is only orange juice. Besides, I put a glass aside for the CO. It's incredible what they don't see when they get their share.

I distribute the glasses to my fellow kitchen staff, all of us taking a moment to enjoy. Big Chris flashes a big smile, saying, "Thank you, Smiley," as he fist-bumps me with the bear paw he calls a hand.

Making my rounds, I distribute the remaining cups, knowing everyone's whereabouts based on the time of day and their routine. Walter in his cube, Sal and Hassan in the shed.

Hassan holds the cup for a moment, breathing deeply and letting it out with a sigh. He holds the glass up to the light as if it were an exquisite Bordeaux. I smile as he tilts his head to the right, taking it all in. "I haven't had freshly squeezed orange juice in six years."

Whoa. I'm reminded of how fortunate I am. I feel guilty for the complaining I've been doing in my head.

Raising the cup to his lips, eyes closed, he takes the first sip. Maybe it's just my imagination but for a split second, he's no longer in prison. The ability to taste, smell, or experience a sensation—to transport us away from ourselves, to another time, if only for a moment. I'd like to think he's home, in his kitchen, with his family. He finishes the cup, a look of peace and contentment on his face.

I didn't think I was doing anything all that special. It's just orange juice. I only wanted to do something nice for my friends.

Sometimes, moments of joy are found in the darkest of places. Sometimes, a smile is more than a smile, and sometimes, orange juice is more than just orange juice.

TWENTY-SEVEN

*"There is something beautiful about a blank canvas,
the nothingness of the beginning that is so simple
and breathtakingly pure. It's the paint that changes
its meaning and the hand that creates the story."*
—PIPER PAYNE

I STILL DON'T KNOW WHAT I WANT TO PAINT, AND I'M OKAY
with it. Painting whatever I want is a little more complicated than
picking up a brush and slapping some paint on a canvas. I've only
painted interiors before and I don't think I'm very good at it. The
painting I hope to create is more nuanced than a roller on a wall.

Before an artist releases their inspiration onto the canvas, they
must prepare it. Under every painting, there is a foundation of
color. Layer after layer of paint, the foundation is what makes
the painting come alive. The artist looks to the vision that the
muse has bestowed upon them and asks, "How do I bring this
to life? What foundation do I need to create to give this gift the
depth, richness, and life it deserves? How will the intersection
of colors interact with one another? White won't be white if I
paint on a blue background."

Crafting the foundation is as important to the finished product as the painting itself.

The same applies to me.

As much as I would like to, I can't just jump into a new life. If, by some miracle, I were to achieve my dreams tomorrow, I'd find myself emotionally where I was before I committed the crime: not feeling as though I'm enough, not feeling worthy of love or success. I'd be a lottery winner who finds themselves broke in two years.

I needed a foundation, and the universe gave it to me that day under the trees at the picnic table. That beautiful and torturous day contained everything I needed.

Love. Family. Friends. Joy. Experiences. Creativity. Honesty. Time. Freedom. Choice.

With a solid foundation, I truly can paint whatever I want.

TWENTY-EIGHT

"In three words, I can sum up everything
I've learned about life: it goes on."
–ROBERT FROST

I'M A GOLDFISH IN A BOWL, WATCHING THE WORLD OUT-
side unfold, unable to do anything with it. I keep up with
current events through TV, newspapers, emails, phone calls
with family and friends, but I can't touch anything. I'm merely
an observer with no connection. And it sucks.

This is the life of an inmate. We watch as our loved ones experience the best and worst moments of their lives—engagements,
weddings, graduations, divorces, sicknesses, promotions, and
firings.

Life is created and life is lost.

I found out my friend Tom died. My neighbor and friend Wayne
sent the obituary via email. Tom and his wife, Barbara, lived
next door. Kyla and I invited him over for dinner one night
while Barbara was away visiting family.

I enjoyed learning about his life and all that he had experienced in his seventy-four years. He was astounded by how many tacos I could eat. I can't do anything except write a letter of condolences on a piece of loose-leaf paper. I wish I could send a nicer card or attend the service. But I can't.

I'm astounded by how complex freedom is. It's much more than being confined for a set period. Watching life unfold as an observer, not as a participant, is isolating. I want to touch, taste, hear, feel life, to engage with it.

But I can't.

I live in a fishbowl. I assume everyone else does too—until I'm on the phone with my aunt, Bobbi. She's so excited about her trip to Egypt, a three-week river cruise down the Nile. She's leaving tomorrow.

"You're going on vacation?"

What about the fishbowl? How are you able to leave? How can you possibly go enjoy yourself with all the crap that's going on? We're in prison.

I hang up the phone, hanging my head in disbelief, wondering how this could be happening. And I learned something.

Life goes on.

Plain and simple, life goes on. There's no stopping it. No matter how much we love someone and how much they love us, life goes on. And there's nothing wrong with it. It doesn't reduce the amount of love between two people.

Life must go on. Each of us has our own life to live. Paths intersect, lives overlap. But each of us has our own life and it's up to us to live it.

Each of us must persevere for our sanity. Moving on does not mean we no longer care about the other's situation. Would I want my loved ones to put their lives on hold any more than they already had? Would I want to inflict more pain by expecting them not to live their lives? The ego screams yes, but the heart says no.

I've been lost in my head, oblivious to others. The world, my family, and friends—all of it is bigger than me. I realize now how self-centered I was before and shortly after the arrest.

We're on this planet, for however long, doing the best we can, dealing with the same shit. It's different shit, but shit, nonetheless. To understand that although whatever we may be going through, and as all-consuming as it may be, others are dealing with the same and potentially worse.

My life must go on. The painting has just begun and I can't stop now.

TWENTY-NINE

"There is an ocean of silence between
us…and I am drowning in it."
−RANATA SUZUKI

I'M STILL WEARING MY WEDDING BAND. I DON'T KNOW why. I'm probably scared to take it off. If I take it off, I'm letting go. And I am not ready to let go. The ring is a symbol of hope. I'm not ready to give up hope. Not yet.

As if wearing it somehow means we're still together. Technically, we are still married, but we're not together. It's been months since she told me that she's leaving me, months since I've spoken to her. She hired an attorney and the divorce is in the works.

She asked me for space, no calls, no emails, no letters. And I'm giving it to her, out of love and selfishness. I hope that by honoring her wishes, I'll get what I want—a second chance.

It's a false hope. I can't fix the damage I've done. It won't go away. No amount of wishing will make that happen. I inflicted a level of damage that can't be undone.

My family asks about her and I have nothing to say. I hate that they ask about her. *Can't they just let it go?*

But why should they when I can't?

I don't know how to. I can't find the strength to take the ring off. I need this symbol. It's the opposite of feeling the handcuffs around my wrists for the first time. If I take the ring off, I make it real. I'm holding onto a past that hasn't existed for a long time.

This isn't even our wedding band, the one engraved with, "You are my favorite." I'm wearing a cheap replacement. I'd lost so much weight that the original band slipped off.

* * *

We're standing in line at an estate sale, the morning sun reflecting off the white vinyl-sided house, my hand in my pocket. I touch my ring finger with my thumb and feel nothing. I panic, reaching further into the pocket, expecting it to be there. It's not. My heart falls through the sidewalk. *Why won't life stop fucking with me? I don't know how much more I can take.*

I keep talking, pretending everything is okay. I don't want to distract us from what we're doing. We have a good place in line. There are only a couple of people in front of us. We need to get what we came here for. Her business has to succeed.

We're done shopping; it's time to head back to the car with our purchases. I can't hold it in any longer. I bend over, hands on my knees, and sob uncontrollably. She walks over to me.

"Craig, what's wrong?"

"My ring—it's gone! I lost it!"

"Let's check the car."

We search the car, but it's nowhere to be found. The one thing I prized among all of my possessions—the one thing that the government couldn't seize—is gone. It was my choice to commit the crime and the consequences of that choice do not seem to have an end. One thing after another, the accident, now this. All my fault.

We couldn't afford to replace it with a duplicate. Maybe we both knew how pointless it would be to even try. We went to Target and bought a cheap ring, one that fit me, as a symbol. We both didn't want me to go to prison without it.

Standing in my prison cube, thinking back to that day and all that I've lost, I stare at the ring. It's been destroyed from working in the kitchen. Whatever luster it may have had is gone. It's dull and scratched. It's turning green and so is my finger.

I have to let go. Holding onto this false hope is causing more damage than good. What opportunities am I unable to seize because my hands are wrapped so tightly around a pipe dream?

How can I move forward with both feet stuck in the past?

I take the ring off, carefully placing it on the bottom shelf of my locker, strategically placed so I can see it when I open my locker. I'm not ready to let it go completely.

I touch my ring finger with my thumb: empty. Like the day I lost the original. There's no panic, only a sense of loss. I don't know what to hope for now.

THIRTY

"If you are going through hell, keep going."
–WINSTON S. CHURCHILL

"HEY, SMILEY, I JUST HEARD THAT YOU GOT A DATE. September 9."

"Seriously?"

"That's what I heard."

I can't believe it. I've been waiting—all of us wait to hear these words. These words mean I'll be going to the halfway house. They mean that I get to leave prison.

I know next to nothing about the halfway house, other than my desire to go there. The halfway house is the midway point between prison and the real world. There is a beauty to the halfway house, the reason I want to go there.

I can leave.

Residents can go to work, church, the gym, doctor's appointments, the laundromat. The thought of experiencing the world again is thrilling.

I had no idea how prison works. I expected I would be living here for a set amount of time and leave on a specified date, that I would know from the beginning of my sentence. Nope. It doesn't work that way. No one knows the date they're leaving prison.

There are so many factors and no one seems to know anything. It's all speculation and rumors. Does the halfway house have availability? Does the prison need the beds for new arrivals?

Half of our conversations in this place are about the halfway house and the longing to hear the words, "You got a date."

These words are the light at the end of the tunnel. We know we aren't here forever, but there is a fear that we will be. Without that date, I had nothing tangible to hold onto. Now I have something and I don't want to let it go. I have hope.

Thoughts are sprinting ahead of me. *Maybe I can get out in time to save my marriage.*

I think about how fortunate I am that one of my prison friends introduced me to his friend, a gym owner. He said he would have a job waiting for me.

He said that months ago. Will the job still be available?

I don't know where else I could work and who would want me.

The relief of knowing the end is near, the sheer and utter joy of knowing this will be over. I can't wait to start the next chapter.

I have to confirm with Mr. Keating, one of the counselors. I knock on his office door.

"Come in."

He's sitting behind his desk, folders and papers everywhere.

"Good afternoon, Mr. Keating."

The lenses of his glasses are so thick, he looks like he is in a constant state of bewilderment.

"What can I do for you? What's your name?"

I know there are 118 of us and that we're a revolving door of arrivals and departures, but I'm in awe that I'm telling him my name for the twentieth time.

"Stanland, Craig."

He looks puzzled.

"I was told that I have a date of September 9. I just wanted to confirm and know what the next steps are."

I feel an emptiness in my stomach as he looks more puzzled. Sorting through the folders and papers, he finds a piece of paper and looks up from his desk. "*Greg* is leaving September 9, not you. It's Greg. Not Craig."

My knees feel like they're going to give out. I'm watching the real world—and freedom—vanish. I say, "Oh. Do I have a date? It's around that time that I should be getting one."

"No. Have a good day."

I walk outside, away from people. I want to cry and I need to be alone.

My friends are supportive. They listen to what happened and tell me what to do next.

"Talk to the camp administrator. It's part of his job to help inmates with their halfway house date."

I'm happy to have a next step, another possibility. But I'm also equally frightened. I think of the run-in I had with the CA and I hope his memory is as bad as Mr. Keating's.

I see the CA by the back door of the common area. My racing heart makes my stomach churn. My freedom depends on this conversation. I can't shake the only memory I have of him.

* * *

It was a beautiful day, so I was training one of my clients outside. He needed help with his conditioning and coordination. I have to be mindful of what I do with him; he's older, weak, and frail. He has a severe curve to his spine and a tremor in his hands. I respect him for showing up to our sessions, for utilizing his prison time to improve.

We were doing step-ups followed by ten alternating punches into my open palms.

I look over my client's shoulder to see a group of men in suits in the parking lot. None of us likes it when the higher-ups are here. They always look for issues and seem to relish finding one. The CA was part of the group and he goes out of his way to find problems, the joy on his face when he does.

He breaks away from the group and makes a beeline toward us. Something is very wrong, but I have no idea what. He is walking toward us as though one of us slept with his wife.

His face is bright red as he screams, "Do you even know what the fuck you're doing?"

I thought it was pretty self-explanatory but keep my mouth shut.

He starts yelling about rules and regulations. Spit is flying out of his mouth as he screams, "Practicing any form of martial arts or fighting is a violation punishable by going to the SHU. Is that what you fucking want?"

I'm starting to realize how bad this situation is. I don't want to go to solitary.

"No, sir."

"Well, I have every fucking right to lock you up."

I'm too scared to speak.

He looks my client up and down several times,

"You're fucking lucky he doesn't look like a fighter. Don't ever fucking do this again or I will lock you up."

I'm praying he doesn't remember any of this as I open my mouth to speak. "Sir, can I have a moment? I'd like to talk about my halfway house date. I don't have a date and others who came in after me are already leaving. I've been an exemplary inmate. You can ask my CO in the kitchen, the camp counselor, and the other CO's. What can be done about my date? My grandmother is very sick; I'd like to see her before she dies. I know that I can get a pass from the halfway house to do so."

He stares me in the eyes and his face turns red. "The BoP doesn't give a shit about your dying grandmother. And if you want to continue to ask about it, maybe you won't get any halfway house time at all."

I've never wanted to punch someone in the face as badly as I do right now. I want to punch him as hard as I can, with the force of the past couple of years. I want to punch him and not stop until I can't punch anymore. But I can't. I can't defend myself. I'm a thing, not a human. And he doesn't give a shit.

Fear quickly replaces my anger. I don't want to piss him off any further.

"Okay. Thank you, sir."

There is nothing to do but walk away. I'm working really hard on turning this around. Why is this all happening now? To taste freedom and watch it vanish.

I'm pissed at my friend. How the hell did he confuse Greg and Craig? Why did he even open his mouth?

Why have I worked so hard in the kitchen this entire time? Why did I bust my ass? For what? I'm going to lose all of my halfway house time and serve the remainder of my sentence here. I feel claustrophobic. Panic is kicking in.

My friends once again intervene and tell me what to do next.

I wrote letters to my family, explaining what happened. My father, in turn, wrote letters to the warden and his congressman. I documented my exchange with the CA in an email to the warden.

It worked.

The warden replied. He made the camp administrator apologize to me and at least ten other inmates for his behavior.

That was nice. But there was something much, much better.

I leave this place on November 9.

THIRTY-ONE

*"Most people talk about fear of the unknown, but
if there is anything to fear, it is the known."*
—DEEPAK CHOPRA

I WALK OUT OF THE SAME DOOR I WALKED IN FIFTEEN
months earlier—through the parking lot, away from the razor wire,
away from the guard towers. Fifteen months confined to a perimeter, I don't feel right on this side of the fence, but it feels good. I'm
not a free man. I'm still property. I'm just property that will finish
the last six months of its sentence in the Brooklyn halfway house.

I see my father, a sense of relief calms my nerves. We shake
hands and hug. It's both an exciting and sad day for him. He
gets to pick his son up from prison but then has to take him to
a halfway house.

As we walk across the parking lot, I look for the car I know,
curious where we're walking. I can't see it. He bought a new car
while I was away. In the sea of vehicles, I don't know which is
his. A reminder that life goes on. It was only my life that was
put on hold.

We reach the car and open the hatch. My clothes are in Uncle Andy's old yellow duffel bag, the badges of the submarines he worked on stitched to the sides. I love that my aunt packed my clothes in this bag. I remember staring at the patches as a kid, running my fingers over the images. Not knowing exactly what my uncle did, but knowing it was really cool.

I can't wait to strip off my prison grays and put on my own clothes. For over a year, it was greens or grays. The greens were mandatory during the day; the grays, reserved for nights and weekends. Everyone leaves prison wearing grays. The greens are returned and recycled for future inmates.

I slide my legs into a pair of jeans and put a sweater on, like stepping into a cozy house with a fire in the fireplace. With this minute action, I feel human again. I didn't know wearing my own clothes could feel this good.

We carve our way down One Mile Drive, my ears popping, the sensation bringing me back to the day I arrived. As I look out the window, the scenery is all new to me, all foreign. If you asked me where I was, I couldn't answer. I'm lost. It's bizarre to live somewhere for over a year and not know where you are.

We reach the highway. I look over at the speedometer. He's keeping it to a modest sixty-five miles per hour. I feel like we're moving at the speed of light and it's freaking me out. I've never experienced car sickness until now. I'm having trouble focusing. As the miles tick by, the weight of reality is settling in. To-do lists running through my mind, nausea adding to the stress.

Prison is a break from reality. The stresses and the harshness of the real world fade into the background. In part, this is good;

it allowed me to do my time. The mental burden of being an inmate is enough. The realities of the world need to be put on the back burner.

Only one problem with that. Everything I put on the back burner is waiting for me on the outside. Issues don't shrink; they grow larger when they're ignored. A laundry list of realities runs through my mind—credit score, taxes, employment, friends, family, finding a home, bank accounts, properties owned, and divorce.

All the unknowns start creeping in. *Will I ever find love again? How do I meet new people? How do I explain where I was? Will I ever have sex again? How do I trust myself after what I've done to my life and the one I love?*

When we exit the highway, I breathe a sigh of relief. We weave our way through the maze of downtown Brooklyn and its insane drivers. I'm not looking forward to walking into the halfway house but I want out of this car. We find a parking spot and I exit as though the car is on fire. I'm relieved to be standing on solid ground but the sensation of moving is still inside me.

I look around at the neighborhood that will be my home for the next six months. Gentrification is all around us—luxury apartments on one side of the street and housing projects on the other. The halfway house blends in; there are no signs announcing its presence. It takes some effort to find the front door. The only marking is the building number: 104.

We ring the doorbell and security buzzes us in.

The moment we cross the threshold, we enter chaos. I squint

as my eyes adjust to the bright lights. Noises are reverberating through the hallway. Someone argues with a guard; others sit on a bench, complaining about something I don't yet understand. The tension in the air is palpable.

As I approach the front desk, I feel overwhelmed. I tell my father, "I got this. You can go..."

"Are you sure?"

"Yeah, yeah. I got this."

I'm embarrassed that I walked into the halfway house with my dad. I watch as he walks out the door. I regret telling him he could leave. I love that he walked in with me, that he wanted to ensure I was safe in this chaos. I think of everyone in my family and how incredible they've been.

The staff escorts me to my room. It's dark and musty, the only light coming from two windows that look out on the designated smoking area. The place stinks of stale cigarettes. There are eight bunk beds with brown lockers next to them. Eight bunks mean sixteen guys, not what I was hoping for—the once-blue carpet, covered in stains, now a shit-colored rainbow. There are several guys in the room, sitting on metal folding chairs or lying on their bunks. They look me up and down, then go back to whatever they were doing.

The staff shows me my assigned bed and locker as they go over the rules. Even with the overwhelm, I'm relieved. I have a place to rest my head and put my things. I make my bed and lie down. The mattress and sheets are even worse than prison. No matter which way I turn, I cannot escape a spring stabbing me in the back.

I stare at the ceiling with no idea what comes next.

THIRTY-TWO

"The art of life lies in a constant
readjustment to our surroundings."
−KAKUZO OKAKURA

I WALK THROUGH THIS PLACE AS THOUGH I HAVE NEVER
been to a store before. There's a sense of urgency on my shoulders, exacerbated every time I check my watch. The lights are
bright and there are too many people, strange sounds all around
me. I don't know where I am in Brooklyn, and I'm a little fuzzy
on how to get back to the halfway house.

The halfway house issues passes for residents so we can go to
the store, church, work, laundry, doctors' appointments, court
appearances, the DMV, the Social Security office. I like that
we're no longer called inmates. Being called a resident feels like
one step closer to freedom.

This is my first full day in the house, my first pass into the real
world. Each pass has a time limit. I have two hours to get my
things and get back. I've chosen to go to the pharmacy for some
basic supplies.

I can't shake the pressure of time. All I want to do is get my things and be back in the house to avoid getting into trouble. The fear of being sent back to prison is affecting my judgment. The punishment for being late is extra work duty, not prison. Doesn't matter. Prison is still too fresh; this fear is real.

Shampoo, conditioner, soap, and toothpaste. That's all I need and yet they're impossible to find. I can't believe how complicated this store is. It's an overly bright labyrinth designed by a crazy person. I'm doing laps around it as if I'm casing the joint. The pressure of time and unfamiliarity blinding me to what is right in front of me. I wasn't gone for that long but apparently long enough to be lost in what should be familiar.

A sense of relief washes over me as I find the aisle I've been looking for, quickly replaced by what looks like an infinite selection. I look at my watch. Is there enough time? I walk to the middle of the aisle for the best perspective. The aisle appears miles long. My mind is creating an illusion that it's bending with the horizon. All I want is Pantene. I'm surrounded by anything but. Looking at my watch, I've lost two minutes standing here. I'm going to be late.

Composing myself as much as I can, I formulate a plan of attack. As if reading a book, I start at the upper left and read to the right, bottle to bottle, shelf to shelf. Apparently, the lunatic that designed the store did not stock the shelves alphabetically.

I find the Pantene, only to be overwhelmed by the million varieties. Why is this so difficult? There's no reason this should be this hard. I follow this process for everything on my list.

With what seems to be the most effort I have ever put into

shopping for shampoo, conditioner, body wash, and toothpaste, I gather my things and head to the register. There is a short line. I stare at my watch as if in doing so, I'll make time slow down.

Reaching into my pocket, I feel the money my father gave me— the soft texture of cotton and linen in my hand. My heart drops to my stomach. Having cash in prison is a significant offense. It means you plan to escape. I question everything. *Am I allowed to have this? Am I supposed to be here? Is all this okay? To be in downtown Brooklyn, shopping, as if I were a free man? What time is it?*

I'm uncomfortable speaking to the cashier. I'm sure she knows who I am and what I've done. I grab my bag and walk out the door. A momentary respite from the lights, linoleum, and over-whelm. Replaced with a new overwhelm: I don't know how to get back to the house. I walk the wrong way for a few blocks and panic about the time I've wasted.

I dreamed of this day for fifteen months, my first foray into the real world. This thing I dreamed of, I cut short by thirty minutes. I'm too afraid of making a mistake, of making another bad choice.

I don't trust myself, even with the simple act of shopping.

THIRTY-THREE

*"The simple things are also the most extraordinary
things, and only the wise can see them."*
–PAULO COELHO

I'M DREADING WHAT I AM ABOUT TO DO. I PAUSE FOR A
moment and stare at the white steel door. The crack addicts are
picking up fragments of crack from the sidewalk, delighted by
what they find.

I have to ring the doorbell to the halfway house, relinquishing
my freedom for the day. I haven't been here long, but I hate this
place. Tasting freedom, only to be confined again, is torture.

Today is different than the other days. My dread mixes with
anxiety. I'm smuggling my iPhone into the halfway house for
the first time. (We're not allowed phones with a camera or the
internet. It's a rule 99 percent of the residents break. This doesn't
make it any easier.)

People have different means of smuggling their phones in. Most
go with a modified jock strap they wear over their underwear,

slipping the phone into the built-in crotch pocket. Some guys earn extra money making and selling these. I've opted for building a false bottom in my backpack, covering it with a pile of gym clothes. Who wants to dig through gym clothes?

I know they are watching me on the camera. I know I can't stand here forever. Resigned, I ring the bell, and the guards buzz me in. Opening the door is the worst part of my day. Once it's open, there's no turning back. I look at the small line of residents in front of me, all waiting to be checked in. We can't just walk in and go to our rooms. There's a process.

I check in at the front desk, signing my name on an electronic pad, which serves as evidence of when I arrived back at the house. Lateness is not tolerated.

We're searched every time we come back to the house. Arms out to the side, the guard runs a metal detector over my body, then frisks me. Deep breath in, I blow into the Breathalyzer. The moment I've been dreading is now. It's time for my backpack to be searched.

I place it on the folding table and empty my pockets. I make sure to put my approved halfway house phone front and center for the guard to see. My thought is, *If he sees a phone, he'll be less inclined to search for one.*

Some of the guards are exceptionally detailed in their search; others don't want to be bothered. My first day smuggling something in, I get the meticulous guard. My heart pounds as he unzips my bag. I don't want my phone taken away. I don't want to get into trouble. Running his gloved hand through the bag, he reaches the bottom. I question my work: *I could have done this better.*

He zips the bag closed. *I made it.* I let the air I was holding in out of my lungs and my muscles relax. This is no way to live.

Up in my room, I carefully pull the phone from my bag. Climbing onto my bunk, I think about where I was just a few short weeks ago. I wanted information but wasn't able to access it immediately. I asked my sister to Google the most ridiculous things: song lyrics, diaphragmatic breathing techniques—she's a rock star and sent me everything I asked for through email or by mailing me printed pages. Accessing the internet through snail mail is bizarre.

Once again, I have the world's information at my fingertips. It's too much. I don't know what to do first—what to look at, what to read, what to catch up on. *What are my passwords?*

Then it hits me. Music. We had a stereo in the gym, but my favorite bands aren't played on the radio regularly. I have not heard Metallica, Black Sabbath, or Iron Maiden in over a year and a half.

Sitting on my bunk bed, phone in hand, I can search for any song I want. Like the Grinch's heart, my world grew three times that day.

I type "'One' by Metallica" in the search bar. I hit the *Enter* key. I close my eyes as I listen to the intro, the faint sounds of war, men barking orders, gunshots, explosions, fading quietly as James Hetfield plays the opening notes on his guitar.

I'm in heaven.

It's like I'm hearing it for the first time. The floodgates have opened. I can't keep up with all the songs I want to hear. As much as I love each piece, I can't wait for it to be over so I can listen to the next one.

I listen for an hour, feeling connected to the world that, only a few weeks ago, was so far away—the pure joy derived from something as simple as music. I feel a swell of gratitude for my sister, where I am, and what I'm doing. I'm humbled by how little it takes to feel joy and abundance.

I'm not physically free. I'm still property. But listening to this music, regardless of where I am, I have found freedom independent from my environment. It's a freedom that belongs to me, always has, and it can't be taken from me.

It can only be relinquished.

THIRTY-FOUR

"People usually are the happiest at home."
—WILLIAM SHAKESPEARE

TODAY'S A BIG DAY, MY NEXT STEP TO FREEDOM. I'M BEING sent to home confinement. My caseworker, Ms. Bruno, wraps the ankle bracelet around my bony leg. It's much bigger than I expected. I don't know how I'm going to hide it. It's still early spring. I hope it doesn't get too warm too quickly. Shorts aren't an option. I'm embarrassed at the thought of people seeing it.

I can't wait to get out of this place. I can't stand it here. I don't like most of the people, neither the staff nor the residents. Most of the staff treat us like shit and some of the residents are still hustling like they're on the inside. When I first arrived, someone said, "Hey, new guy."

Prison made me wary of my fellow inmates and their motivations. I maintain a safe distance between us. "Yes?"

"You doing laundry today?"

"I am. Why?"

"You should know there's a park across the street from the laundromat. You can take the steps to the top and sit on one of the benches while you wait for your clothes. This way, you don't have to wait in the laundromat."

Wow, that wasn't so bad. I don't know what I was expecting but it wasn't a recommendation for a beautiful place to sit.

"Thank you, I appreciate it."

"You know, a lot of people would pay for information like that. Like $10."

And there it is.

"Let me understand something. People would pay to hear that there's a giant, tree-filled, green park across the street from the laundromat? I hope you find some of those people because I'm not one of them."

I can't wait to get away from this place.

I will only have to deal with them once a week when I check in to the halfway house to pay them their money. They get 10 percent of my gross. Another two months and I'm done with that too.

It's amazing I even have a place to go home to. My ex-girlfriend Lysia stepped up massively and has subleased her apartment to me while she's working in Seattle. I'm not sure where I would have lived without her kindness. I was not kind to her. Her forgiveness fills me with shame but I'm grateful for it.

My credit is shot and I have no money. I couldn't have lived anywhere else. My family helped me financially and a friend inside prison was able to hook me up with a front-desk job at a gym. Even with that, I wouldn't be able to live anywhere else. Lysia helped save me.

I leave the halfway house and walk to the apartment. The BoP utilizes defense satellites to monitor us. As I walk down 7th Avenue, I look to the sky, wondering where it is. I feel it looming overhead.

The walk is teaching me a valuable lesson. I have to wear two socks under the bracelet. I have three blocks to go and I'm not sure I can make it. This thing has rubbed my ankle raw. This is one of the worst limps I remember having. Can I hop on one leg for three more blocks? The pain is so terrible, this seems like a viable option.

I walk into the apartment. I don't feel comfortable calling it my apartment. It feels very temporary and I fear losing it before I even live in it. It feels foreign. I open the closets to see Lysia's clothes. I feel like I'm invading her space.

I walk around, check out the bathroom. Then it hits me. I can take my first real shower.

I strip my clothes off, thinking how nice it is to stand naked and alone as I wait for the water to get hot enough.

I step into the tub, my bare feet touch the porcelain. It's a pleasure that's indescribable. I've worn shoes in the shower for eighteen months. Hundreds of guys using a handful of showers that are cleaned sporadically by fellow inmates who are made to do the work, not because they want to. Hundreds of guys, pissing, spitting, jerking off. Shoes were not a nice idea. They were mandatory.

The water pressure of a real shower, the privacy of an actual shower curtain. No more rape-prevention shower curtains, transparent from the knees down and chest up. I can't look out, and no one can look in.

Water is water, but this water is warmer and somehow richer. Being alone and not being watched is the luxury of taking my time.

I dry myself with big, soft, wonderful towels. I walk barefoot through the apartment. I didn't know I would be this grateful to be barefoot—the beauty of the smallest of luxuries.

It's time for bed. I pull back the sheets and comforter. I'm used to climbing up to the top bunk. I feel like I'm lying on the floor. The sheets are soft and cool, the pillow is normal sized and not lumpy. The memory foam mattress topper feels like a cumulus cloud.

My bedroom door is shut. It's private. It's quiet. It's my first night's sleep in a real bed, wearing nothing but boxers and a T-shirt. There's an unwritten rule for inmates: we don't sleep in underwear. We wear shorts over them.

There are no other conversations. There's no snoring. There are no jingling keys from the CO's. There is only me and my thoughts.

I'm unsettled by how quiet it is. It takes a long time for sleep to come.

THIRTY-FIVE

*"It is not the man who has too little, but the
man who craves more, that is poor."*
–SENECA

IT'S ONLY WEDNESDAY. WHY IS FRIDAY SO FAR AWAY? IT
needs to be Friday. I need my paycheck. I don't have enough
to pay bills, to live, to eat. The walk home from work is cold.
My hands are numb, a reminder of reality. Gloves are a luxury
I can't afford. I'm tired of living paycheck to paycheck. I'm tired
of the same thoughts every two weeks.

When is that bill due?

When is my next check?

*I hope the guy at the deli who sells me chicken cutlets for $1.50 is
working. I can't afford the $2.50 the other guys charge.*

I did this to me. This is my life now.

That last thought wraps its tentacles around me, pulling me

into the past, back to a time when things were perfect. When life was comfortable. When I wasn't wearing an ankle bracelet. I could buy anything I wanted, whenever I wanted. Comparing past to present, the present doesn't stand a chance.

Remember when I made in a month what I now make in a year?

Remember when money wasn't a problem?

Remember when I was somebody?

God, I want to go back in time. I want to feel the security of having money. I don't want to choose between a MetroCard and a chicken cutlet for $1.50. The MetroCard always wins. I have to go to work, I need the hours. Work means food in the future.

I can't believe I did this to my life. I can't believe I work the front desk at a gym, making $12 an hour. It's embarrassing.

What would my old job pay me on an hourly basis?

A few quick calculations, and I'm sick to my stomach.

The shame that this is my life, the shame that I fucked up my life and that I will never be enough. I had perfection and I destroyed it all.

Thankfully, my mind steps in and saves me. That last statement doesn't ring true. The past was far from perfect. I wasn't comfortable. I was in the same boat I'm in right now.

Life wasn't easier. I was living paycheck to paycheck. The paychecks were bigger and so were the bills. I was spending more than I was making. Each month, I stressed how I would pay the American Express bill and keep a roof over our heads. I wondered how I would maintain a lifestyle I was growing tired of and that was killing my marriage. It was the crushing weight of maintaining an illusion, the lies, deception, and energy required to keep it alive. It was exhausting.

I was consistently living in the future, spending money I did not have. Commission checks were spent before they were received. I was daydreaming of the next grand purchase so I could fill the void, if only for a moment. I was missing all that was in front of me and available to me—my marriage, my family, and friends.

I didn't own my things. I was a slave to them. I was a slave to always needing more. I lived in a prison I did not see.

∗ ∗ ∗

Reaching the front door of my apartment, a wave of gratitude washes over me. I stand on the threshold, looking at the apartment I live in. I smile at how beautiful it is and that I can call this home.

None of the furniture is mine. I own some plates, a lamp, an iPad, and the clothes I wear. I don't care about what I own. I have shelter. I have a box of cereal. My hands are warm. I think about where I was and where I am. I think about the people I have met, the experiences I've had, and the adventures yet to come; moments in life that do not cost a dime.

The magic of kissing someone for the first time, that incredible moment of anticipation right before our lips touch. The magic of the thousandth kiss. Holding someone's hand. Saying, "I love you." Time with family and friends. Athena sitting on my note-book, purring, chewing my pen. Staring at the horizon. The sound of the ocean. Hiking an unknown trail. Experiencing the sunrise and sunset as a free man. The freedom of choice.

With less than I have ever had, I have all that I need.

THIRTY-SIX

"He only earns his freedom and his life Who
takes them every day by storm."
−JOHANN WOLFGANG VON GOETHE

I PLACE MY RIGHT FOOT ON A CHAIR AND PULL MY PANT leg up to my calf. I stare at the ankle bracelet for the last time. Two months of wearing this clunky device, two months of being tracked by a satellite, two months of my bony ankle being rubbed raw. No more. Today is the day it gets cut. Today is the day I become a free man. My caseworker, Ms. Bruno, struggles with the safety scissors.

With one final clip, my ankle is free. I'm free.

The amount of paperwork leading to prison is tremendous—financial disclosures, the PSR, more DNA tests than I can count, fingerprints. Now, with a snip of a scissor and one signature, I'm a free man. I'm not complaining but it was a little anticlimactic. I thought maybe confetti would fall from the ceiling or a marching band would play. I don't know, just more than one snip.

I'm astounded by how good my ankle feels as I walk out of Ms. Bruno's office. She smiles and says the same thing she says to everyone in these moments, "Good luck, Mr. Stanland. Don't come back."

I walk past the same commotion I experienced six months ago when my father and I first walked in—still the same complaints, only with different voices. I don't have to live here anymore. I don't have to come back. I don't have to piss in front of the guards every week.

Each step feels amazing. Each step is a step closer to what I have been dreaming of. I push open the door I despised pulling open. I don't turn around as I hear the door close behind me. I shut my eyes for a second. The spring sun is warm on my face and my heart fills with joy. With freedom. With choice.

I'm not the property of the US marshals. I'm not the property of the Bureau of Prisons. I am as free as I have been in three years. I can choose whatever direction I want.

There was only one thing I wanted to do and nothing is stopping me from doing it. I walk through downtown Brooklyn, each step further away from the worst time of my life. With each step, there's a whisper of doubt.

Am I allowed to be doing this?

Where do I have to be? What time do I have to be there?

Is my ankle bracelet sufficiently charged? I need to ensure my phone is charged so I can call the halfway house when I arrive at my destination and when I'm leaving.

Freedom is a new concept, one my mind is struggling with.

The universe sends me a reminder: a piece of graffiti on the Manhattan Bridge, and all it says is *Freedom Forever.*

I look to the sky and say, "Thank you."

My stomach growls, as I've been too excited to eat. Many of the guys at the halfway house pushed their ankle bracelet boundaries, going a different way home, stopping in stores. Not me. There was no way I would do anything to compromise my freedom. There were countless times I'd walk by a restaurant or a bodega, my stomach screaming for food. Pausing at the window, peering inside, like Tiny Tim staring at the Christmas turkey. I never walked in. I was too afraid to deviate from my path.

I smile as I walk into the first deli I see. I order a coffee and croissant. The first sip of coffee is delicious. The croissant flakes in my hand and melts in my mouth. This is the best meal I've ever had.

My dreams for this day were all the same. Find and be near water. Water calms me; it brings me peace. I was fortunate. The halfway house is a short walk to the Brooklyn Heights Promenade. This is precisely what I wanted. A quarter-mile stretch of boardwalk with what I think are the best views of Manhattan. It's early May and the tulips are in bloom. I stare at them as I walk toward an open bench, taking in their brilliant oranges, yellows, and purple. I sit away from the tourists, enjoying my coffee and croissant.

The East River is busy with ferries, barges, jet skis. The Brooklyn Bridge in the not-so-far distance is reflecting the afternoon sun.

I have nowhere to be and no one to report to. I can just be. I feel lost without the pressure of time, like I'm supposed to be doing something. I don't know what, though. I allow myself to settle in, sitting and staring at the water, remembering this is what I've been dreaming of.

I decide to walk home, toward the bridge, through Dumbo, stopping every so often to take it all in. Without the bracelet, I can stop as often as I want and for as long as I want without a schedule to keep.

As I walk into my apartment, something is different. Something is missing. The watchful eye of the satellite is gone. I'm not a prisoner to the ankle bracelet and its demands.

It required charging twice a day, tethering me to an outlet like a dog on a leash. I no longer have to fear the halfway house sending a signal to it, causing it to vibrate, always in the middle of the night, always scaring the crap out of me. I don't have to sleep with the anticipation of the nightly phone call confirming my location.

Every night the phone rang between the hours of 1 a.m. and 4 a.m. I would answer the phone in a daze and mumble, "Stanland, Craig: 22052-014. I'm home." Click.

I was a prisoner to the phone. I walk into my bedroom and unplug it from the wall. I carefully wrap the cord around it and place it in a drawer. That phone will never ring again. I have the freedom to sleep through the night. I breathe a sigh of relief. My apartment feels bigger, and I still feel a little lost. Then, something dawns on me, and I have an incredible thought.

I grab a jacket and walk out the front door.

Because I can.

THIRTY-SEVEN

*"To keep the body in good health is a duty...otherwise we
shall not be able to keep our mind strong and clear."*
−BUDDHA

IT'S BEEN A MONTH SINCE MY RELEASE FROM THE HALF-
way house and my newfound freedom is settling in. I still
question whether or not I can leave my home. *Will someone be
looking for me? Am I breaking the law?*

In an instant, fear rushes in. It's the fear of going back, fear of not
wanting to make a mistake. Fear of walking out my apartment
door. It's an awful feeling. I come back to reality. I remember I
am free. I remember I can walk out of my apartment without
permission.

I leave my apartment building and look around. Running shoes
tied tight—one foot in front of the other. My pace is slow, my
muscles tense. My Achilles heel throbs, a prison injury, making
itself known with every step. I foolishly attempted to touch
the bottom of the basketball net and it had left with a physical
manifestation of a past I'd like to leave behind.

I start down 7th Avenue and take a right up the hill toward 8th. I cross over 8th and decide to head toward 9th—a spur-of-the-moment decision. Arriving at what I expected to be 9th Avenue, I realized there is no 9th. It's Prospect Park West. I'm not sure where I am. My sense of direction is notoriously bad. Faced with a choice of right or left, I choose left. In a few short blocks, I find myself at the entrance of Prospect Park.

I'm surprised that I live this close to the park. I had no idea. I am excited that my world has expanded exponentially. A reminder not to take for granted the choice to go left or right and the things we can discover when we let go.

I love parks. Always have. I love being out in nature. I enjoy the city but miss the suburbs and their openness and woods. To experience the sounds of nature and the elimination of man-made noise. Connecting to something more significant than myself. I'm grounded, centered when I'm alone in nature. It's a reminder of how beautiful the world is. A reminder of how small we are. A reminder that we're all connected.

I run into the park, unsure of what to do with my newfound discovery. My mind is still set within the confines of routine. Trying to process the possibilities of my expanded boundaries. Even with freedom, I find myself trapped. The mind is a powerful prison, its bars imaginary yet so strong. Fears, insecurities, the shadow of the past, the glare of the future.

As I explore this new world, a pine tree catches my eye. One of its branches runs parallel to the ground—nature's pull-up bar. My workout begins. Pull-ups, push-ups, dips on park benches, jump squats by the softball field, bear crawls between light posts. Focusing on each pull, each push, each step and jump. My heart is pumping, my lungs are sucking up air. Sweat drips in my eyes, and my shirt is sticking to my chest.

There are no prison walls. There are no bills to pay, no anxiety, no divorces, no money troubles. The past and the future cease to exist.

It's only me. My mind and body are a unified entity with a single goal: the completion of another rep. Feeling the blood flow to the muscles as they work. Each rep a victory. Each rep a mantra keeping me focused on the task at hand. The outside world ceases to exist. I feel no pressure.

I'm within a bustling city and yet alone in the woods. Not afraid of being by myself. Quite the opposite. Embracing myself, feeling at ease with the pain. The pain that only exercise can bring and the pain that those who exercise crave. The last rep complete, my breath returns to normal, veins popping from my arms. A massive sense of accomplishment.

I set off to explore the park. With no agenda, with no idea where I am going, I take rights, lefts, this path, that path.

I was always happy when I'd feel a kick to the bottom of my prison bunk. This was Hassan's signal that he was handing something up to me. I loved it when I saw his hand holding the *New York Times*. I skipped the news and went straight to the lifestyle and travel sections. Taking notes in my journal, I recorded a bucket list of places I wanted to see and experiences I wanted to have when I was free.

There was an article about Prospect Park, its history, things to see and do. One of the highlights was the unknown waterfalls hidden within the park. I love waterfalls, getting lost in the sight and sound of falling water. This is the number-one item on my bucket list. It doesn't cost any money, I love waterfalls, and it's an easy thing to cross off my list.

Walking up a narrow pathway, I hear something and think to myself, *There's no way. I can't be on the verge of crossing an item off my list this early in my freedom.*

My ears follow the sound as my pace quickens. The path leads me straight to it. Set back from the sidewalk, the surrounding woods have grown so that the falls are naturally framed by them. The water cascades down the granite rocks into a small pool below. The trees, clouds, and sun reflected on the surface are like a near-perfect mirror.

I sit on a bench and think about where I was a year ago at this time. Wishing for death, no freedom, my lowest point. Now I live ten minutes away from a place I dreamed of seeing with the knowledge that my wish for death was a wish to escape a temporary situation. Sometimes it's good we don't get what we think we want.

I walk home, enjoying the new neighborhood. There is a brown-stone covered by trees, a small fishpond in the front. The sound of the water trickling down makes me smile. I realize that I have the freedom and choice to take this time and admire it.

I will do this again but not the same way. A different path, a different routine. Ruts are easy to get into, more challenging to get out of. Best not to get into them in the first place.

The journey back to who I am and who I want to be is a long one.

Today was a step. Move the body, expand the mind. Embrace freedom in all its forms. There are still more prison cells I need to walk out of. Right now, I am grateful to be walking out of this one.

THIRTY-EIGHT

"An animal's eyes have the power to speak a great language."
—MARTIN BUBER

EVER SINCE MY ACCIDENTAL DISCOVERY OF PROSPECT Park, I've made it part of my routine. Returning home from my yoga practice, enjoying Windsor Terrace, my mind is a constant flow of thoughts.

I stand on the shore, watching them pass. Until that one thought, that one dark thought comes floating along. The river stops as if frozen in time. I feel helpless as I watch the scene unfold. I can't escape it. It's too strong.

The sky in my mind grows dark, the sun obscured by clouds of sadness, self-doubt, fear, and unworthiness. The winds develop with tornado-like force, destroying everything in their path. My feet are cemented to the ground and I'm forced to watch the damage take place. My world shrinks as the clouds grow heavy and fall to the ground. I'm surrounded, the cold fog clinging to my skin.

I'm sad, filled with self-doubt. I'm not worthy of being loved, being happy, experiencing success, or forgiving myself. I question all that I have done and all that I dream of doing. My inner dialogue is a torrent of shit: *Who do you think you are to achieve your dream, with what you've done?. You're incapable. You can't trust yourself, how will anyone else?*

My relaxing yoga practice in the park is a distant memory. I shake the thought off but the damage is done. Fear, sadness, self-doubt, emptiness, and unworthiness consume me.

I think about all I have studied and read. I remember that I'm not my thoughts. I think of every hack, tool—anything to snap me out of this funk. The brain senses this and tightens its grip around my thoughts. The more I fight, the deeper I go.

It's as though my mind wants to be this way. It wants to feel sad, content to walk through the wreckage.

Shame tells me I have to pay a penance for what I did. A battle between wanting to snap out of it and wallowing begins. Wallowing is winning. Fear, sadness, self-doubt, and unworthiness are just too powerful.

I resign myself that today is just going to be one of those days.

I return to my apartment, grab a bottle of water from the fridge, and place Athena on the kitchen counter. She settles herself on the corner of my notebook. I take a seat on the wooden stool, our morning routine begins.

Her purring vibrates through the countertop. She chews on my pen as I attempt to write. I never know if she's helping or casting criticism on my work. The words are flowing but the shadow of self-doubt is in the ink of every word. I stop writing and look into her big, green eyes, thinking, *Cats are the only creatures that can be this comfortable and content.*

I feel a surge of guilt for leaving her for two years. She was in good hands but I left her. Now, sitting on the counter, she holds no grudge. She is present in this moment. No past, no future. I can learn from her.

My heart swells. The grip of fear, sadness, self-doubt, and unworthiness is releasing. I realize there are no tricks, hacks, tools, or things that can be learned from a book to pull me out of the black hole of guilt and shame.

There is only love.

Love for another, love for myself, love for an animal. To paint whatever picture I want, there must be love.

THIRTY-NINE

*"A mind that is stretched by a new experience
can never go back to its old dimensions."*
−OLIVER WENDELL HOLMES

THE CLOUDS MOVE QUICKLY ACROSS THE SKY AND THE
fall sun feels good on my face. I take a deep breath. Salt in the
air and the earthy aroma of beach roses ignite my mind with
memories. It's been years since I have smelled these smells. It's
been too long since I have seen the ocean. I still can't quite
grasp that I'm hiking the Cliff Walk in Newport, Rhode Island.

A year ago at this time, I was in prison. My freedom was nothing more than a memory. Within the confines of those walls,
I couldn't imagine being able to do this. To envision a future
where I could experience beauty such as this. It didn't seem
possible.

I dreamed of vacations, the inside of my prison locker plastered
in stunning scenery. It was a tour of the world: glaciers and
waterfalls in Iceland; the summit of Mt. Kilimanjaro; Devils
Pool in Victoria Falls; rows of vintage cars lining the streets set

to compete in Mille Miglia, a thousand-mile race across Italy; the Tolkien-like stone bridges in Watkins Glenn State Park.

Every time I opened my locker, a moment of possibility was quickly replaced with the voice of doubt, reminding me it was only a dream. I learned to look but not touch. Vacations were an impossibility. No money. No freedom. Criminal.

I remember the afternoon when this became my reality. Alone in my cube, staring at the floor, conversations all around me, a thought rushed into my mind. It was as real as anything: *I will never go on another vacation. I will never again be able to go out to dinner. I will never experience either of these with someone again. It's impossible.*

Another consequence of my actions, guilt consumed me. I thought about Zach Braff's character in *Garden State*, climbing onto the excavator at the edge of the quarry, rain pouring down and screaming. Screaming as loud as he can.

I get it. I dream of climbing to the top of something, anything, and screaming. Letting it out, the sadness, the guilt, the shame. I thought if I had the opportunity, I could scream it all out, but it's impossible.

I see a precipice just off the trail, jutting out from the cliff. It's begging to be climbed. My muscles adjust, muscle memory kicks in with every uneasy step. Focusing on the goal, the need to reach this point consumes me. Catching my breath as I get to the top, I take in the scene.

I stare at the green-blue waves of the Atlantic a hundred feet below me. Breaking at various points, moving at different speeds, creating different sounds. Within all these differences there's a consistency. The sound of the ocean, always changing, always the same. My heartbeat slows to its cadence.

I think back to that day in my cube, staring at the floor, convinced I would never again be able to enjoy life, including the simple act of standing on top of a cliff and staring at the ocean. I believed it. It was real to me. I thought how badly I had wanted to scream, to take all the shit that was inside of me and scream it all out. Screaming would make it all better.

Right now, I have no desire to scream because all I can think of is, *I'm doing the impossible.*

FORTY

*"Nothing is permanent in this wicked
world, not even our troubles."*
−CHARLIE CHAPLIN

I HAVE A RECURRING DAYDREAM, A WISH FOR MYSELF.

I travel back to prison and observe myself from the outside. I'm like a ghost, floating above the cement walls, across the room from my cube. The guards have just completed the ten o'clock count. I watch as I climb into bed and settle into the sheets. I know what comes next. I know what he's feeling.

I hear the whispers in his mind, the begging, pleading, and praying: *Please make it fucking stop.*

Over and over until sleep puts him out of his misery.

I want to float across the room to comfort him and share what I've learned. I want so badly to tell him, "The pain that is consuming you is temporary. I promise you this. Everything may seem lost and that you have nothing left. This isn't true. You have family and friends who love you. That hurt you feel? Take that pain, multiply it by a hundred, and place it in your loved one's hearts. Know that it will live there for the remainder of their lives. This is what will happen if you choose to end your life. You will be responsible for that.

"You have the power of choice. Don't take that for granted. It is the greatest freedom you will know. Even ending your life is a choice. Contemplate the power behind that.

"This experience will transform you. It will provide you with one of the greatest gifts life has to offer—the peace that comes from emerging from the bottom. The knowledge that you can endure. The wisdom to know that whatever may happen, as painful as it may be, it's temporary. These gifts do not dissipate with time. They are yours for life and they grow like weeds when you water them.

"Life is perpetual transformation, always evolving, circumstances changing. Give yourself one more day. It's impossible to know what can happen tomorrow if you're not around to see it. Ask yourself, *Do I really want to die or do I not want to feel like this anymore?*"

This is my daydream and yet I have no control over it. I'm stuck on the other side of the room—watching and wishing. I understand he'll have to figure it out on his own.

Emerging from the ashes is a necessary component of the journey. This is where the gift is born.

I may not be able to speak to him but I can live these words, remembering how close I came and how beautiful life is because I didn't.

FORTY-ONE

"A straightforward, honest person should be like someone who stinks: when you're in the same room with him, you know it."
—MARCUS AURELIUS

AT WORK, I FIND MYSELF IN THE MIDDLE OF MY SALES PITCH, the same spiel I've given a hundred times before. It flows now without my even thinking about it. The customer asks the same question almost everyone asks, "Is it busy when I plan to work out?"

I don't want to lose the sale. I don't want to face my boss if I do. My default mode takes over. I tell the same lie I've told hundreds of times before, "No, it's not busy when you plan on working out…"

The words leave my mouth effortlessly. The lie is automatic at this point. This time it's different, though. As the words pour out, my body fights back. My heart tightens, my stomach grows uneasy, I feel weak. Not only physically but mentally.

This is not the man I want to be. This is not how I want to live. It's not sustainable.

This is the day I understand the damage I've done to myself. A lie as insignificant as, "No, it's not busy when you plan on working out…" chips away at the man I aim to be and the man I've worked hard to create.

In the physics definition of integrity, an object has integrity when it's whole, when it's undivided. I wouldn't want to live in a house that lacked integrity. I'd be living in fear, always wondering, *Is today the day the roof caves in?*

How can the same not be said for my body and mind? When I lie, I voluntarily give away a piece of my self-sovereignty. I've experienced and suffered the consequences. I know what happens. No wonder I didn't believe I was enough or worthy. I had chipped too much away. I was living with no integrity.

When I lie as a means to an end, like selling a gym membership, I taint the very thing I'm pursuing. I place my desire, my goal, above the person I'm lying to. I make myself and my outcome more important than whomever I'm speaking with.

I take away the equality we share as human beings. I demonstrate a lack of respect for the other party and for myself. When I lie to get what I want, I water and fertilize the very essence of what I struggle with: that I'm not enough or worthy of getting what I want without lying for it.

When I lie to avoid an outcome, I'm attempting to manipulate a predetermined fate fear has fabricated. I've decided that, without the lie, the result is scary, uncomfortable, and something worth avoiding at all costs. Lying destroys the present moment and constructs an anxiety-filled future. Lying eliminates possibilities. It shrinks my world.

When I was lying to myself, to Kyla, to my family, it was like juggling. There were so many balls in the air. My life was focused on keeping the balls in the air and the fear of letting one of them fall. This isn't living. It's a form of imprisonment.

Even with this knowledge, I still lie. Fear wins, I fall into the trap of short-term comfort. Fortunately, my body responds every time I do and I learn to observe the lie and the reasons behind it. What am I avoiding? What am I scared of? The answers to these questions are the direction I need to go in.

To paint whatever I want, there must be freedom. Freedom can be found everywhere, especially on the other side of integrity and honesty.

FORTY-TWO

"If you're to create something powerful and important, you must at the very least be driven by an equally powerful inner force."
—RYAN HOLIDAY

I REMEMBER SITTING AT MY DESK IN ELEMENTARY SCHOOL, like many schoolchildren, staring at the clock. I had watched as the second hand moved backward before it moved forward and asked myself, *How is that even possible? Is it three o'clock yet?*

Two of the slowest experiences a person can endure: waiting for three o'clock and prison.

My teacher's voice droned in the background. I understand where Charles Schultz found the inspiration for the voice of Charlie Brown's teacher. I passed the time by daydreaming, thinking of what I would do when I got home. *Should I expand my LEGO village? Race my remote-control car, drive my go-kart?*

Whatever was waiting for me, I couldn't wait to get home and work on it. Regardless of the toys, there was a theme they shared. Everything had to be built, then played with, customized, refined, and tested. The building was as fun as the playing.

My schoolbooks were filled with drawings and doodles, my imagination running wild, crafting stories to share with my friends. Designing car engines and full-blown cars. Whether something was physically possible didn't matter. I created without reality getting in the way.

Ever since I was a child, I've been at my happiest when I'm creating.

The gift of a blank canvas has me back doing what I love. Creating, writing, building, designing, coming up with ideas. I wake up early, giving myself the gift of time before I have to go to work.

Rebuilding is exhilarating, understanding that I'm the architect of my life. Some days the words, thoughts, and ideas flow. It's magnificent. Other days, not so much. But like that kid, I love the building, not the outcome.

> Inevitably, in the middle of my enjoyment, a voice alerts me. Calling everything I'm doing, working toward, what and who I want to be, into question.

In her book *Radical Acceptance*, Tara Brach shares one of the Jataka tales, the stories of the Buddha's previous lifetimes.

> A merchant is tending to his shop when he sees a beautiful and luminous being walking across the town square. The merchant's heart lit up from the compassion he could sense emanating from

this man. He knew he wanted to serve this being and give his life to awakening such life in his own heart.

The merchant carefully prepared a tray of ripe fruits and tea to offer as nourishment and walked out of his shop. As he crossed the town square, mindful not to spill the dish, the sky turned dark, and the earth opened up. Lightning and thunder tore through the clouds. Demons appeared all around him, eyes of evil and mouths filled with blood. He heard the voice of Mara, 'Go back! Turn around! It's too dangerous. You won't survive!'

The sky grew darker, thunder and lightning, louder and brighter. The ground beneath his feet shook and opened, fire spewing from the cracks. Mara continued the tirade of fear. 'This way is not for you! Who do you think you are? Go back to your shop, to the life you know.'

Ugh. The first time I read the words, a chill went down my spine, my stomach churned, I shrank from the page. I've heard these words in my own mind, along with too many others: *you will fail; you don't know how to do this; you're not good enough at [fill in the blank]; you're not enough; you're not worthy of love or success.*

For too long, I listened to this voice, allowing it to rule my life. Succumbing to the fear and the doubt, going back to the life I know, keeping what I love out of reach, merely a fantasy. Better to dream and never try than to try and fail.

One day I heard another voice alongside the voice of doubt and fear. It spoke from deep within. It spoke with confidence, saying only one word, *Enough.*

The voice was unwilling to deal with doubt and fear any longer. I knew I had to capture the fear, to shine a light on it. Word for word, I transcribed the voice of fear and doubt, catching it in real time.

This will never work; you've got no experience; who would buy this?

As I wrote, the fear grew. It felt counterproductive to capture it.

Am I adding fuel to the fire? Does writing it down make it real?

The voice that said, *Enough*, also said, *No. See this through to the end. Push through.*

What happened next was unexpected. As the pen moved across the page, the crushing power of the thought vanished. The voice of doubt and fear, once crippling, had no weight, no substance. One word flowed naturally as I finished writing: *Why?*

The once-mighty voice of doubt and fear had no answer. There was no supporting evidence to substantiate these statements that were only moments ago drowning me. All the crap, the negative self-talk, exposed. I shined a light on what held me back, only to find it doesn't even cast a shadow.

I've made this a practice, referring to it as "Spotlight." Whatever I'm doing, when the voice of doubt and fear start speaking, I immediately stop, go to the margins of my notebook, my phone, whatever I have handy and write the word, "Spotlight," and allow the fears to pour out—no edits, no holding back, a stream of conscious pouring onto the pages.

The most challenging part of the practice now is to transcribe the thoughts to their end. I don't need to. Their power vanishes before I complete the sentence.

Why? is repeated over and over as I write, eroding every ounce of substance the thought once had. I have found it's critically important to get it all out. If the voices of doubt and fear want attention, I give it to them. I turn the light on as bright as it will shine.

Keeping a record of the Spotlights, patterns form. Old beliefs and thoughts hardwired in my mind. I see what needs work, what needs attention. What direction I need to go. I see the prison cells I've created and that I must walk out of.

There is a second half to the story of the merchant.

> As the ground shook and Mara continued to instill fear in the merchant's soul, the merchant almost succumbed. He was terrified. And rightfully so. He thought about turning around, listening to the voices. But at that moment, his heart swelled with a longing so great it could fill the entire universe. This desire for love and freedom was stronger than any voice of warning. He continued in the face of great terror.

> One step became two, then three. The demons disappeared, the earth reassembled, the sun emerging from the clouds. Reaching the luminous being, the merchant was trembling with aliveness. The great being embraced him and said, "Well done, bodhisattva, well done. Walk on through all the fears and pain in this life. Walk on, following your heart and trusting in the power of awareness. Walk on, one step at a time, and you will know a freedom and peace beyond all imagining."

A feeling of pure joy washed over me when I read this. I looked up from the book and said, "Holy shit, I just discovered the secret to life."

FORTY-THREE

"The shortest answer is doing the thing."
−ERNEST HEMINGWAY

I WANT TO EXPERIENCE WHAT THE SHOPKEEPER EXPERI-
enced but fear is suffocating. Betraying my voice, going against
my better self, has eroded the inherent trust I believe resides in
all of us. No trust only compounds my fear.

I don't blame my voice for leaving. I wouldn't keep talking to
someone who ignored me, told me they were so much smarter
than me, and treated me like shit.

I miss my voice. I didn't understand how important it is, how
much I need that voice to live. The torture of self-mistrust is
excruciating. Second-guessing every choice, feeling empty inside.
Without trust, I'm finding it difficult to rebuild. Rebuilding from
scratch requires confidence. No self-trust equals no confidence.

A while back, a friend tweeted, "The surest path to self-
confidence I know is making and keeping commitments to
myself."

It stuck with me. Having confidence in myself means I trust myself. I brought it up to him a year after he wrote it. He thanked me for reminding him. I thought it strange that he'd forgotten. It's how he lives his life. I realized it's his natural state. He has internalized it, like brushing his teeth. When a practice becomes ingrained in how we live our lives, it runs on autopilot in the background—our life runs through its filter.

I think of his words as I stand outside the glass conference room, my heart racing. Observing the people inside, they share a familiarity that triggers my insecurity.

"I'm the outsider," I mutter to myself.

A two-year process boiled down to this moment. I'm debating whether I should walk through the door. I don't have to walk through the door. I can turn around and go home. No harm, no foul. Except I made a commitment to myself. My friend's tweet rings in my ears. I have to learn to trust myself and if I fail to keep this commitment, I never will.

When I started the rebuilding process in prison, I examined what landed me there.

Fear.

Fear of being honest, fear of appearing unable to support our lifestyle, fear of being seen as less than. I'm responsible for what I did but fear was the fuel.

This realization led me to write down my fears, so I could see them laid out in front of me. I wanted to see what was holding me back.

My number-one fear was easy to identify. I've had it for as long as I can remember. I've also harbored the secret desire to master it. It's interesting how the thing that scares us the most is the very thing we need to do.

I was good at my job. Very good. Always in the top three. Plaques, accolades, trips to Hawaii, the whole nine yards. A few times a year, the company held sales meetings and every meeting began the same way. One by one, each account executive would state their name, the office they worked in, and their client demographic.

"Craig Stanland. Stamford, Connecticut. My client base is compromised of the largest financial institutions in the world."

That's it. That's all I had to say. I would rehearse the statement over and over in my head like a mantra. I panicked as my turn approached. My heart racing, my armpits and chest sweating, my stomach churning. It was awful. Speaking in public scares the hell out of me.

Here I am, standing outside the Premier Toastmasters Club in downtown Brooklyn. Every Google search yielded the same result, Toastmasters, an international organization focused on speaking in public and leadership skills.

It's taken me a year to attend this meeting. My excuse machine is running on overdrive. I don't have the time, I don't have the money, I have nothing to say, I'm not worthy of attending the meeting, I have no skills. It's probably an exclusive club that wouldn't want me as a member.

I reached my breaking point. The pain of not acting outgrew

the pain I feared. I wanted my voice back. Remembering my commitment, I walk through the door and introduce myself to everyone. I sit as far away from the podium as possible.

The host of the meeting asks for volunteers to speak. In an instant, I'm back in the corporate world, at the quarterly meeting, anxiety screaming at me. The mind and body pulling out all the stops, full panic and protect mode: heart racing, sweating, stomach churning.

Miraculously, my right hand shoots up in the air. For a split second, I wonder who the heck did that. Walking to the front of the room, I take my place behind the podium. I'm surprised how different the room looks from this vantage point. Like a magician, the host fans a deck of cards in front of me, saying, "Pick one."

I grab one from the middle and hand it back to her. She reads the question printed on the flip side. The podium is mine for the next two minutes.

All eyes are on me and they are filled with anticipation. I speak for twenty-six seconds, stumbling through an answer with no idea what I said. I don't know if I was coherent or if I even answered the question.

With a warm round of applause, I go back to my seat and sit down, my heart racing, sweat still pouring. I feel a massive shift taking place in my body—energy surges. I feel alive. It's pure, unadulterated joy. I faced my biggest fear and did not die.

It doesn't matter what I said or if I made sense. I did it. That's all that matters.

When I experience art that I love, in whatever form it takes, there's a depth to it. I feel as though I can swim in the paint, dive into the words on the page, float in a river of musical notes.

The artist went deep within, trusted themselves, faced their fears, and put it out in the world for all to see. They made a commitment to themselves to not leave anything behind. The courage behind the vulnerability is what separates the good from the extraordinary.

I want to apply this to my life. This is how I want to live with what time I have left. Rebuilding trust, rebuilding confidence, it's not easy. They are a product of experience. And experience is the product of action.

I understand that the voice never left. It's been with me the entire time. I just wasn't aware of it. It was there when it said, *Enough*, when it said, *What can I do?* The more commitments I make and keep, the more I reconnect with what was always there.

The more I can rebuild and reinvent.

FORTY-FOUR

*"Some of us think holding on makes us
strong; but sometimes it is letting go."*
—HERMANN HESSE

I'M EARLY. I'M ALWAYS EARLY. I PEEK INSIDE HER STORE.
It's more amazing than I could have ever imagined. I see Kyla,
my heart skips a beat, a surge of emotions washes over me. I
have to remember that it's all in the past. Our only connection
is what once was. She's my ex-wife and I'm her ex-husband.

The end of love is a puzzling thing. How something so big,
beautiful, and all consuming can vanish so quickly. Time and
distance turn lovers into strangers.

She's engaged in a conversation with someone, I'm assuming
a customer, or is he something more? Old habits kick in, the
emptiness of jealousy fills my stomach. *Who is he?*

She sees me and smiles. I smile back. I'm hoping she lost her
ability to read my face.

I don't want to disturb her. This is awkward enough as it is. I walk around her new truck as she finishes her conversation. I remember when she called to ask for help finding it and asked for help negotiating with the dealer. I was useful once again and it felt good.

I'm surprised by how nice it is and by how big it is. I picture her driving it. I'm impressed.

As I walk around from behind the truck, she's done talking and waves me in. I open the door to the smell of lavender. It's warm and inviting. We hug. What was once passionate and filled with electricity is now nothing more than a hug reserved for acquaintances. Not too tight, with a respectful amount of space between us.

We were texting a few weeks back, wrapping up some loose ends with the divorce, when we decided to meet for drinks. I've been in a state of anxiety ever since then and I hope that doesn't show either.

Since I'm no longer property, I can drink alcohol again. It's not like it used to be. It's not as much fun as I remember—the feeling of losing myself, becoming someone new with each sip. I don't like it.

She introduces me to the guy. He's one of her employees. I feel stupid. She takes me on a tour of the store, telling me about the projects she's working on. I flash back to the flea market; her eyes are filled with the same passion and excitement. It's a far cry from the business she started in our one-bedroom years ago.

The tour complete, she asks, "So where do you think you want to go?"

I think about the time we spent in this neighborhood. We had a lot of fun here. I don't know why I was so scared of this place.

"How about that place with the horseshoe bar? I always liked that place."

"We can do that. Do you mind if I walk Matisse before we go out?"

I was afraid to ask if Matisse was still alive. I'm happy she is and that I will get to see her.

"Of course not."

We walk down the street, past where the pop-up shop was, past the businesses I already knew about, and the new ones I've never seen. She tells me all about the new stores and what is going on in the neighborhood.

We reach her building. "Do you want me to wait outside?"

"No, you can come in."

I remembered when I was only a few weeks into my stay at the halfway house. I came to pick up some clothes and a belt she was holding on to for me. I really needed the belt. I didn't have money for a new one and I was sick of my clothes falling off me. She met me on the street with two brown paper bags. She wasn't ready to let me in her home—that hurt.

We walk into her apartment. It's small but the high ceilings make it feel big. I feel out of place, like I'm walking into a different life in a different world, one I'm not a part of but one I wish I were.

Matisse walks over to us, a tear fills my eye. I'm so happy to see her. I don't say anything, but she is so skinny, so old. I kneel to her, cooing, "Hey, baby girl! You're so pretty."

She leans into my body. It feels good. I can't tell if she remembers me or is just happy for the attention.

We walk slowly. Matisse walks with the stiffness of age. I know it's a part of life but it's breaking my heart. We bring her back into the apartment and get ready to leave. Matisse looks at us with the sadness dogs have when they are on the wrong side of a closing door. This is probably the last time I will ever see her. This time I know it's true.

The restaurant is a short walk away and it's almost empty. It's just before 6 p.m., so happy hour hasn't started. We grab two open seats at the bar and order drinks quickly. The first round goes down fast and we order the second round as quickly as the first.

We catch up: family, work, friends. The more we drink, the deeper we go. We get into what happened between us.

She has resentments and rightfully so. She goes back to a day in our bedroom, long before the arrest. It had come to the point in our relationship where we had to discuss having children.

Kyla and I were the best of friends before we started dating. She knew my stance. I had always said I didn't want them. She did. She had to ask a question that had a 50 percent chance of disappointing her.

"You've said you're unsure if you want children or not. I need to know: are you leaning toward having them or not?"

Here at the bar, second drink almost finished, she recounts my reaction. "You said you were leaning toward not and you rolled over and went to sleep or pretended to go to sleep. You treated me as a thing. You didn't treat me like your wife or your friend. Your answer wasn't wrong; it's how you did it and how you treated me."

I regret that day. I regret how I hid behind fear.

She looks me in the eyes and says, "You want kids. You know you do."

I lie. I want her back, so I give her the answer I thought she wanted to hear. "You're right. I do."

The words don't feel right coming out of my mouth. I take the coward's way out again.

I'm not lying when I look at her and say, "I still love you."

A glint of anger flashes in her eyes, transforming to sadness. She inhales deeply, pausing before she speaks. "I met someone. His name is Andrew. We've been together for ten months. I'm going to marry him."

My expression doesn't match the words coming out of my mouth. "I'm happy for you. You deserve to be happy."

It's time to part ways. We hug with space between us.

The subway ride home is filled with the things I wish I hadn't said. *Why did I lie? Why would I do that to her? Have I learned anything? I don't know why we did this, why we met up. This was pointless and painful.*

The thought of hurling myself in front of the next train flashes through my mind. Shame running rampant that my mind still goes to that place. Haven't I moved past that?

✶ ✶ ✶

I wake up hungover and confused. My head is killing me and the sheets are soaked with sweat. I feel disgusting. I check my phone: one missed call from Kyla at 2:30 in the morning.

I text her, "I saw the missed call. Is everything all right?"

Apple's empty text bubble appears as she types.

"It was nothing."

"You sure? Calls at 2:30 in the morning aren't usually nothing. We should talk."

"It's fine. Talk about what?"

"Us, what we talked about last night. Unresolved issues."

"We are over. There is nothing more to talk about."

I debated before replying. I was hurt. I wanted to know what she wanted to say to me. I had a hope that it was an "I want you back" phone call.

Still holding onto a pipe dream. I know her well enough to know it wasn't that and that she would never tell me what was on her mind.

Anything left unsaid would remain left unsaid. She has someone, and that sucked, but I needed to move on as well. I had to.

I hesitate as I type the words, walking around my apartment nervously, rereading our messages, expecting something to magically appear that will help guide me as to what I should say.

I hit the send button.

"It's probably for the best if we don't speak again."

"I agree."

"Good luck with everything. I wish you well. Let me know when you make it into *Vogue*."

"Good luck to you as well."

FORTY-FIVE

"I learned that courage was not the absence of fear, but the triumph over it. The brave man is not he who does not feel afraid, but he who conquers that fear."
−NELSON MANDELA

PRISON TAUGHT ME THE VALUE OF TIME, HOW PRECIOUS, how short, how once it's gone, it's gone forever. I think about what was behind my actions and choices. What was the root cause of losing precious time?

Fear.

Fear is a door that appears on the path when a choice must be made. No house, no walls, no supporting features. Just a door in the middle of nowhere. It reminds me of an abstract Dali painting. Sometimes I imagine a melting clock and tortured souls off in the distance.

I can't see what's on the other side of the door. It opens to a new and unknown world. And that's what scares me. My imagination tells me what's on the other side and it's never anything good. Fear tells me everything I don't want is waiting for me on the other side. There is guaranteed pain and suffering if I cross the threshold.

The door is so easy to avoid. Why would I possibly walk through it? I understand the temptation the merchant felt, of going back to the path he knew, the safety of the known. My life will be fine if I avoid the door. Nothing would change.

Therein lies the problem with avoiding the door. I don't want fine. The gift of a blank canvas is far too incredible to settle for fine. The foundation is coming along, I am rebuilding trust, and it's becoming a bit of an addiction. Living an extraordinary life, a life on my terms, painting whatever I want, will not happen if I avoid the door.

How much more of my life am I willing to sacrifice to fear? I've lost more than I care to think about already.

The first time I went skydiving, I was filled with equal parts of excitement and panic. Sitting at the opening of the plane, the wind hammering my face, the ground twelve thousand feet below. The instructor strapped to my back, counting down, "Three, two, one..."

We leap into the abyss. The first thought is, *I don't want to do this anymore!*

Walking through the door is horrifying. Leaving certainty for uncertainty. It's not sane. I wished I were back in the plane. I could not un-ring this bell; I was fighting a losing battle with gravity. I questioned my sanity. And then it happened. It was nothing short of magical.

Every time I walk through the door, I'm transformed. I see fear for what it really is—nothing more than a complex and often beautifully crafted tale spun by the imagination. No substance, only words. Allowed to run wild, fear will dictate my choices and, in turn, my life. Fear is the story I believe that prevents me from growing.

The magic happened as I was racing to earth at 120 miles per hour. The terror disappeared. It transformed into adrenaline and the immediate desire to make another jump before I even touched the ground—the thrill of the free fall combined with the peace of floating gently to the earth. The view of the planet we live on from this perspective is incredible. This experience will be mine forever.

The door doesn't only appear for the "big" fears like jumping out of a plane or speaking in public. Life is filled with small challenges, mini doors. I'm finding that the choices made in these moments are the foundation of life.

Telling the truth when the lie would be easier. Having a challenging conversation when avoiding it is an option. Looking beyond the perceived short-term comfort of an easy choice and focusing instead on long-term fulfillment. Living with integrity and honesty. Choosing to be vulnerable. I'm learning how much freedom can be found in saying, "I'm wrong. I made a mistake."

Fear is a compass pointing me in the direction I need to go. I don't always follow it. I certainly don't walk through every door. It's a practice. The more I practice, the more freedom I earn.

FORTY-SIX

"We suffer more often in imagination than in reality."
−SENECA

"PLEASURE TO MEET YOU. I'M CRAIG."

"So nice to meet you. I'm Anushwa."

Her dark hair and eyes contrast with her bright orange dress, her brown skin bridging the two. I'm in awe of her beauty, doing my best not to turn into a stuttering, stammering buffoon.

We speak throughout the night. The conversation flows. She exudes energy and her eyes speak volumes. With each word spoken, I grow more intrigued.

Earlier this week, I decided to put relationships on the back burner. I have shit to do and I must focus on it. I've found what I want to do and I love it. The satisfaction of pursuing work that is meaningful to me fills me from the inside. I feel energized and focused.

But this woman, this beautiful and exciting woman, chances like this are rare. I decide to go for it; I'm going to ask her out. The second I make this choice, the door appears. My heart is telling me to walk through it, grab the doorknob, and go. I know there is something great on the other side.

My ego isn't having it. It's fueled by fear and is utilizing every tool in its tool belt, seductively calling me to the safe path. *C'mon, take the easy route for the rest of the night.*

I ignore the voice but the ego doesn't give up so easily. Fear is far too powerful to quit this early.

She's out of your league. Save yourself from the humiliation.

Then, *What are you thinking? You just said you have shit to do. You don't have time for this. You have work to do.*

That's a good trick of the ego, using something I love against myself.

You don't have the money to take a girl like that out.

Here's an interesting one. My mind has judged this woman without knowing a thing about her. Purely by appearance, my mind has deemed this woman wouldn't be interested in a man without money. So how much is enough anyway? The ego isn't sure, only that I don't have it.

You'll have to tell her you're a convicted felon.

Ugh. I'm still not comfortable with this being a part of my story.

If she says yes to a date and we hit it off, then yes, I will share my history with her. I hate that I have to do this, that this is a part of my life now. It's not how I want to be seen. But I remember what happens every time I share the story.

I walk through another door. I feel energized. A wave of inner peace comes over me, one derived from the confidence of knowing I am not my past—the power of owning the story versus being owned by the story.

I am the man I am now because of the gift I received from making this mistake. Not one person to date has judged me poorly for being a convicted felon. If anything, I instantly become more attractive.

The ego ignores this. It only knows doubt and fear, showing me the easy way. Ego presents a path filled with rainbows, waterfalls, and unicorns sipping water from a creek. Funny, I don't recall the trail looking like that before I decided to ask her out. The ego is a master magician, creating illusions that are both appealing and frightening.

The path of asking her out only has a door on it. I can't see what is on the other side. I have no idea what's beyond that door. But fear and ego do. The broken pieces of my self-esteem, humiliation painted on the walls for all to see. The path has become the fire swamp from the *Princess Bride*, brimming with danger and rodents of unusual size.

She disappears. I don't see her for an hour. My mind is doing two things simultaneously—rejoicing that I won't have to humiliate myself and my self-esteem will remain intact. And

I'm equally disappointed that I missed my opportunity. A juggling act between the two.

She walks back into the room, backpack on, ready to leave for the evening. My heart skips a beat. I didn't miss my opportunity. This is it. Now or never. I pick one foot up, followed by another. My ego is screaming, *Where are you going? Don't do this!*

I approach the door, reach for the doorknob, and turn it slowly. I walk through and it happens. I stepped outside of fear and into a place of power. A place where action trumps outcome. I say the words with ease, no trepidation, with the confidence I gain every time I walk through the door. "It was a pleasure meeting you tonight. I would love the opportunity to take you out sometime."

I'm on the other side. There is no fire swamp. There is no humiliation. My self-esteem is intact.

Walking through the door is a path to freedom. Crossing the threshold creates opportunities and possibilities. The outcome is no longer what matters. The effort I put in, committing to action, rebuilding trust within myself, this is what matters.

"Thank you so much for asking, but I have a boyfriend."

Lucky guy.

FORTY-SEVEN

"I set out on a journey of love, seeking truth, peace,
and understanding. I am still learning."
—MUHAMMAD ALI

I STAND AT THE WATER'S EDGE. THE OVERCAST SKY DIF-
fuses the sun's rays. I have to squint to see. The December air is
cold and the wind is steady. A lone seagull rests on the seawall,
her white feathers fluttering in the wind. Waves, no higher than
my knees, break on the shore with force. Nature is showing her
strength and within that strength, her beauty.

A woman feeds stale bread to the seagulls, a feeding frenzy
ensues. The last of the food dispersed, she retreats to the warmth
of her car. A lone gull lands on the hood, stamping its webbed
feet, as if demanding more. I smile. She is one of a few at the
ocean today. The others remain in their cars, reading a newspaper or book. They're occasionally looking through their
windshields at the beauty that's before them.

I'm the only one standing in the cold. The reason I came rests
firmly on my shoulders. A place I've never been, but a connec-

tion I feel. Aunt Bobbi made this his resting place. A place they shared, filled with love, laughter, and the stolen moments that make life, life. His soul touched the ocean, now forever a part of it. Returned to the earth.

Three days ago, I heard the call to come here. A dream I cannot remember but the message was clear. Three days to question, to doubt, to build expectations. Ignoring the logical, choosing instead to listen to my heart, I find myself standing before him. So much has happened. I feel empty, lost. I had to see him. I need to ask for his forgiveness.

He died on July 19, 2008. He fought for years against a debilitating disease. But he battled, knowing the inevitable, he resisted. He fought the way he lived, with dignity, courage, and honor. The disease slowly took away his body but could not touch his soul.

The end was near. Phone calls were made and we gathered by his side. It's a simple room. It will never be anything more, nor does it desire more. Memorable for not being memorable. Details fading into the background, wallpaper for the events that unfold within them.

I walk to the bed, my uncle sitting upright for his comfort. I approach him, the disease rendering him paralyzed and unable to see clearly. My aunt tells him I'm here. His central nervous system devastated, his body a prison. Despite all of this, he smiles.

It's the smile I've known for all these years.

This was the uncle I knew. His spirit broke free of the prison his body had become. That smile is one of the most meaningful moments of my life.

We sat and waited, exchanging small talk to sidestep why we're here. Waiting for something we spend our lives in fear of. Something we try so hard not to think of and yet it dictates how we live life. In moments of love and pure unselfishness, we secretly wish it for those closest to us who are suffering. We let go of our need for them in our lives so that their lives can be better.

There was nothing more to see or to do. I was dating Lysia at the time and my family told us to go home. The drive home was filled with stories of him, memories. Lysia was amazing, her support, her love. We walked into a dark house, the only light coming from the answering machine.

That light was a messenger beckoning in the darkness, speaking volumes without uttering a word. He died while we were driving home. I sat on the living room floor, knees to chest, and wept.

I wish he knew how much I loved him, how much I respected him. He died long before my crime, but I know he's been watching. I think of him often. Shame and guilt for my actions rise to the surface. An overwhelming feeling of disappointment carves a hole in me. I fear that I let him down.

I know he loved me. I know he would have supported me. I know he would have continued to love me regardless of my crime. I know all of this, yet the emptiness remains. What I carry is my own.

My aunt spread his ashes in the water that crashes before me. She loves him with all her heart and he loves her with all of his.

She tells me stories, things I never knew about him. Characteristics I didn't know but wasn't surprised to hear. Handwritten love letters left for her to find. No occasion, just because he had to share what was in his heart.

The little yet grand gestures that couples cultivate over time. Intimate moments shared between lovers and friends that build a foundation of love and trust. The knowledge that, no matter what, with this person by my side, it will all be okay.

The time had come for her to let go, not of love, but of his earthly remains. She chose this place. A place woven into the fabric of their lives. She spoke to him as she spread his ashes atop the ocean. The sun shone down, reflecting on the water. At that moment, he came to her. The dance of the waves and the light of the universe became one and his face appeared within the ashes. His spirit, living free, visited earth once more.

His last smile for her.

Now I stand in front of him. Staring at where the earth and the sky become one. I don't know what to say, how to begin. I'm alone yet self-conscious. The voice in my head fills me with doubt. It's telling me this won't work, this was foolish, I should be working. I should be anywhere but here. Being busy. Productive. Unrelenting chatter echoing through my brain.

The voice of fear disguised as doubt.

The heart and mind battle. Emotions are rising, consuming my body. I feel like a balloon on the verge of popping. My mind seeks shelter from what I'm doing to myself. A small voice, a child's voice, offers me an escape. Run away. Go home, leave this place. Leave the emotions behind. We can tuck them away, stuff them in a box in the corner of the attic with the rest of the clutter.

The sun breaks through the clouds. The warmth of its rays touches my face. I come back to where I am. The ocean is alive with light. Flashes of brilliance dance to the music of the sea. Each wave plays a different note, each ray of light dances its own dance. All of them beautiful, hypnotic. There is a rhythm in the randomness. Within that rhythm, I find the courage to speak.

"Hi, Uncle Andy."

My words are unsteady, spoken through a veil of shame. All I can manage is small talk. Banter reserved for strangers to seem polite. The voice of doubt and fear ring in my head. I look within. This isn't why I came here. My heart rises above the noise and lets its voice be heard. At first a trickle and then a raging river. The words and tears flow.

I tell myself this is three days of anxiety and expectations. Three days manifesting to this moment. I know this is false. This moment began the moment the FBI left that voicemail. Over three years' worth of shame, guilt, and self-loathing. All of it pouring out.

"I fucked up, I fucked up; I'm sorry. Please forgive me. Please talk to me…"

Tears and snot dripping down my face, I plead with all my might for a sign. "Please let me know you hear me, I need something, anything. I don't know what to do, I don't know how to move on. Please…"

As I wait for a sign, I pause long enough to look where I am. To be present in this moment. This place is beautiful. It is peaceful. The weight of coming here obscured how gorgeous this place is. I know he would be happy here. I start walking.

My eyes take in all that is around me. Some of the homes are boarded up for the season. A jetty divides the water in front of me. The sand is coarse and laden with rocks. The waves pick them up and move them with every break. An added layer of sound, the symphony of nature growing deeper.

My begging and pleading evolve into a conversation. I speak with him like we're back at the dining room table for Thanksgiving dinner. I always sat next to him. I tell him about Kyla. It makes me sad they never met. "You would have really liked her…"

I keep talking and he listens.

A stone, no different than any other, catches my eye. I pick it up. Resting it in my palm, I stare at it. Round and smooth, millions of years wearing down any edges. Small pockmarks dot its surface. I think of its time on the planet and how now it has found its way to me. Or how I found my way to it.

The words come out, without thought, without a filter. Just free.

"This is the past. This is the cage that is around my heart. This is everything that is holding me back. This is everything that keeps me from moving forward. This is what is preventing my heart from feeling love. This is preventing me from forgiving myself. When I let go of this rock, I let go of my past. I open my heart to love and forgiveness. I open myself to now and the beauty of this moment."

I look at my hand. My fingers are wrapped tightly around my past. Afraid to let go of what has become my identity. I've allowed my history to become who I am. Too scared to find out who I am when I let go of who I have become. This must change.

I draw my arm back and throw the stone into the ocean. With a satisfying kerplunk, it breaks the surface and gradually finds its way to the ocean floor. I think, *Where will it be in another hundred million years?*

I feel relief but not the absolution I had been hoping for.

As I walk to the bluff, I see an orange rock and yellow shell. The rock is bright and stands out among the many. The shell is pearlescent and glowing in the sun. I pick them up. I declare the stone as the present. The shell represents love. I don't ever want to let them go. I already know where I'll put them in my apartment. Next to my bed, always in view. A reminder of this trip.

I reach the top of the small cliff. A rock, jutting out, sits high above the water below. I climb out and rest. The view is fantastic from up here. The length of the beach in view before me. A tree, dead for many years, clings to the cliff face out of sheer determination. Its gray branches twisted and warped by the ocean breeze. I feel safe and at ease as I share some last words with him. I said what I needed to say. And he listened. I decide to leave.

As I walk to the car, I see something out of the corner of my eye. There are rocks, hundreds of them, forming some kind of pattern. I want to investigate this further.

The voice returns. I should leave this place. I have things to do, emails to reply to, I have to be busy. So much to do. Get in the car and go. The voice is whispering that I can see it next time. It reassures me that I will make this trip again and that whatever this is will still be here. Choosing an unknown future instead of the here and now. The future that so often scares me is now a better choice than the present.

The same energy that brought me here tells me to ignore the voice. It feels good.

A pattern comes into focus as I approach. Someone has meticulously placed, not hundreds but thousands of stones below the bluff. Circular patterns, beautiful and purposeful. There is a small sign, sealed in plastic to protect it from the weather. The paper faded from the sun. It takes a moment for the words to come through.

The Meditation Labyrinth: An Ancient Seven-Circuit Maze.

The instructions are clear. Be present as you walk, make your way to the center of the maze. Be present with the twists and the turns, the rocks that make up the path, the sand beneath your feet. Set your intention. What is it you seek to release? Anger, grief, sadness? Or what would you like to celebrate? Joy, happiness. Letting go.

I stand at the entrance. I take a deep breath of the salt air. I set my intention: the dream, the anxiety, all of it sitting at the forefront of my mind.

I follow the maze slowly and deliberately. Looking at the stones, feeling the sand beneath my feet. Stopping to look at the water and to see where I am. Here. With him. Eventually, I reach the middle of the sculpture, which is the end of the labyrinth.

Looking at the rocks at my feet, I know what to do. I pull the orange stone out of my pocket and place it gently on the center stone. The present is not something to hold. Each moment is one to embrace, then let it go. There must be room for the next moment.

My heart speaks. Let go of the yellow shell, let go of love. I know I have to. I know it is part of my journey. I take it out of my pocket. The sun shines through it, making it glow in my hand.

I'm thankful to have known this shell in all of its beauty. It is the most beautiful shell in the world. I'm grateful I was fortunate to have it in my life, even just for a short time. Carefully, I place it atop the present. I smile when I think of the next person who will enter the labyrinth and see it to the end. Maybe they will pick up love and hold it for a little bit.

I retrace my steps back out of the maze. The instructions stated when you exit the labyrinth, you leave like a new person. I believed it. Maybe it was hope—attachment to something I see but can't touch. Pausing at the exit, I breathe in the ocean air. Taking my final step out of the maze, it's as though I have stepped back into reality.

There is no weight lifted. I'm not a new man. But maybe there's more. Knowledge and understanding. The wisdom that forgiveness comes from within, that I hold the key. It's always there. It's just up to me to turn it. There are more labyrinths to walk, more challenges, more adversity.

I stand to face the ocean. The sun, falling lower in the sky, is still warm on my face. Its reflection on the ocean's surface is stretching to the horizon.

"Goodbye, Uncle Andy. Thank you for calling me here. Thank you for this day. I love you."

FORTY-EIGHT

"When you forgive, you in no way change the past—but you sure do change the future."
–BERNARD MELTZER

FORGIVENESS ALLUDED ME ON THE BEACH THAT DAY. I wanted it so badly, I needed it. I wanted to hear my uncle's voice riding on the back of the breeze, telling me, "Craig, you are forgiven."

With his forgiveness, I could forgive myself. Without it, I don't know how to. I'm trapped by this belief: *I'm a terrible person, unworthy of anything good.*

These words wrap around my heart and choke me from the inside. Their grip is powerful; I don't know how to break free. The freedom I've learned to love, to embrace, that I'm floored by every single day, is incomplete. I know there's more.

I will never be free unless I forgive myself.

I am friends with a beautiful, incredible woman; watching her evolve has been an extraordinary experience. I love having her as a friend; she challenges me, she inspires me, she makes me laugh. I'm a better person because of her. I love our friendship, but I dream of more. I want to tell her how I feel, but I don't. Partially out of fear, but mostly the belief that I'm not worthy. I'm not worthy of feeling anything more; I'm not worthy of her feeling more toward me.

When I think of her, the butterflies flutter. I love this feeling. It's part of what makes being alive so incredible. It only lasts a short time. Unworthiness takes over and shuts it down. A small piece of me dies every time I do this. I'm trapped by shame and the inability to forgive myself. Shame is an insidious disease that will eat me alive if I don't learn to forgive myself.

* * *

In his book *Love Yourself Like Your Life Depends on It*, Kamal Ravikant asks the question, "If I loved myself truly and deeply, would I let myself experience this?"

Of course not. No. Never.

If I loved myself has become a vicious cycle. I don't love myself enough to forgive myself. I can't forgive myself because I'm not worthy of love for what I did to love. Round and round it goes. I want off this ride.

Sitting at my desk, a beautiful spring day is just beyond the sliding glass doors. My balcony, huge by New York City standards, stares back at me. In the morning, incredible views of the sunrise. In the evening, the sun sets behind the Statue of Liberty. The green oxidized copper cast against a canvas of oranges, pinks, and purples. Outdoor space in New York City is one of the most prized commodities one can hope for in an apartment. My balcony is spectacular.

And it goes unused. I don't go outside. I only look at it through the glass. I'm not worthy of it, a self-imposed penance to pay for what I've done.

When I made the trip to see my uncle, I was asking for something I wasn't ready to give or accept. I didn't get what I was seeking, but I realize the gift I was given. The courage and self-worth to make the trip. The awareness to listen and trust my heart.

Staring outside, the sun peeks over the apartment buildings, she pops into my head. She does this quite a bit: her smile, those eyes, her voice. The butterflies are awake and they begin to flutter. I don't shove the feelings aside. I don't dismiss the butterflies. I don't know what makes this time any different versus any other time, but a question comes to me: *How am I ever going to forgive myself if I'm not worthy of sitting outside on a balcony I pay for?*

Forgiveness is not a concept to be learned. It's an action to be taken. Knowledge without action is philosophy. Without effort, without genuinely examining my beliefs, I don't think there would ever be a limit to my suffering. It would continue in perpetuity. I will carry this burden, which I imagine will only grow for the rest of my life.

The answer was simple. I purchased a four-piece patio set from Amazon. It arrived in pieces and I loved every second of putting it together. There's an old wooden chair in the corner that has been passed from tenant to tenant. Nobody thought it was nice enough to keep. A fresh coat of navy-blue paint brings it back to life.

I examine my handiwork, it's awesome. But something is missing. I scout my neighborhood, hunting for anything my neighbors have put out on the street for others to take. I hit the jackpot two doors down, a window box and a clay pot. I fill them with lavender, thyme, and purple flowers I don't know the name of.

My work is complete. I feel energized and tired all at the same time. I sit in one of the chairs. It wobbles a lot. I think of how cheap the set was and accept the wobble as an endearing, quirky trait. I love what I've created. It's more than a balcony. It's an opportunity. To move forward, to take another step, to stop punishing myself for what cannot be changed.

Extending an act of kindness to myself does not make me an evil person. It's quite the opposite. It makes me the person I want to be.

FORTY-NINE

"In every walk with Nature one receives far more than he seeks."
—JOHN MUIR

THE SIGN COMES INTO VIEW. I MAKE THE LEFT-HAND turn, driving slowly through the rusty gated entrance. The sound of gravel beneath the tires makes me smile—I flash back to driving my go-kart on our gravel driveway. I park the Mini and walk to the kiosk. The Mianus River Gorge trail map is laid out in front of me. Where is the trail I'm looking for? Which one will bring me to the waterfall? This is why I came here today—to find the waterfall. I see the path I came in search of and my hike begins.

Tributaries flow down the hillside, carving their way to the river in the valley. The elevation is no higher than 500 feet. It would be a stretch to call it a hike, more like a nice walk in the woods. The first buds of spring add a splash of green. The forsythia are like yellow bonfires sprinkled across the hillside.

Alone on the trail, the sound and pace of the city is a distant memory. Instead, I hear the orchestra of Mother Nature—water flowing over rocks, the birds emerging from their winter solstice. The treetops sway in the gentle breeze.

I ignore the "Trail Closed" sign and walk around the barrier. I hear the waterfall before I see it, my heart skipping a beat in anticipation. Walking up and around the bend, I find myself directly at the top of the falls—a sense of satisfaction in reaching my destination.

I enjoy this perspective for a moment before looking to the bottom. I see where I want to go. Nature has generously provided a seat to take in her glory, a branch, the height of a short stool running parallel to the ground. I watch as the once-raging water transforms into a mirror of calm.

I look at my cell phone, no signal. I smile, a moment of solitude. I feel gratitude for being here and for enjoying a part of nature. I'm grateful I have the money to rent a car, the freedom to experience this adventure, an impossibility not that long ago.

The sensation of gratitude fades. As it wanes, I feel a sadness filling the void. Then, like a dam bursting, it washes over me. I'm drowning in it. I know it was always there, running in the background. It was patiently waiting for a moment of silence to be heard. A fist closed around my heart the day I was arrested and now its grip is tightening. I'm helpless.

The experience is too powerful. Fighting it would be pointless. I hand myself over to it. Closing my eyes, I invite the sadness in, allowing it to course through my body. It's the sadness of the past. I'm consumed by regrets and judgments of things that cannot be changed. I never fully processed any of it. Memories run silently in the background of my mind, dictating my life without my conscious knowledge.

Intuition takes over, telling me what I need to do. Forgive.

I forgive myself silently, a gentle whisper in my mind. I forgave the seven-year-old me for being scared of the dark. I forgave the twelve-year-old me for not punching the bullies who tormented me that hot summer afternoon. I forgave myself for the lies I've told when the truth would have set me free. I forgave myself for the dreams not pursued and the projects not finished. I forgave myself for the women not spoken to. I forgave myself for believing that I am not enough. I forgave myself for not having courage. I forgave myself for not loving myself. I forgave myself for not listening to my heart. I forgave myself for the pain I caused Kyla and my family.

Forgiveness flowed like the waterfall in front of me. As it flowed, it transformed. Forgiveness for myself morphed into forgiving others. I forgave those bullies. I forgave the girl who called me a loser in front of the seventh-grade class. I forgave people who rejected me. I forgave the prosecutor, the lead investigator, the judge.

Eventually, the forgiveness peters out. I sit quietly for a moment, taking in what just happened. Trying to reconcile how memories I haven't thought of in over thirty years bubbled to the surface with ease. Experiences I would have sworn I had let go.

Once again, intuition took over. I breathed in six deep belly breaths. With every inhale, the smell of nature, a radiant light, the water from the falls. With every exhale, whatever was trapped inside me.

Let go of...

Hatred.

Fear.

Insecurity.

Jealousy.

Shame.

Exhaling the sixth and final breath, I open my eyes slowly. The forest is transformed: colors are brighter; sounds are sharper; the smells are cleaner. It's euphoric.

In this magical moment, a dull yet powerful pain emanates from the center of my chest. It scares the hell out of me. I wonder if my moment of enlightenment is being cut short by a heart attack. I think about the miles between me and my car. I remember that I have no cell reception. The irony doesn't escape me that only moments ago, I was celebrating the peace of being alone. My fear grows with the mounting pain.

I close my eyes, I let the pain in. I don't know what else to do other than embrace it. This pain is nothing to fear. Finger by finger, knuckle by knuckle, the fist clenched around my heart is slowly releasing its grip. My heart has room to breathe, for the first time in a long time. It's adapting to its newfound freedom; my heart is stretching its legs.

Opening my eyes, I stare at the waterfall, taking it all in. My body comes alive. Energy is flowing through my veins. The shame running silently in the background has been replaced with a sense of peace and comfort in my skin.

I decide it's time to explore the rest of this beautiful place. I stand up, practically launching myself from my seat. I'm as light as a feather. I've been carrying the seven-year-old me, the twelve-year-old me, all the past versions of myself for all these years.

I've been carrying the pain that exists only as a memory. Nothing is ever forgotten. All of it was stored in my subconscious mind, running silently in the background. Haunting the present moment with the ghosts of the past. Just because I don't think about the past doesn't mean it's not there. I don't think about the air I breathe. This doesn't make it any less real.

Forgiveness is a journey—one of acceptance, of loving myself, of knowing I am enough and worthy. When the memories arise, and they will, I hope the memory of this day reminds me of what I need to do.

Forgiveness is freedom, and freedom is everything.

FIFTY

*"When we meet real tragedy in life, we can react in two
ways—either by losing hope and falling into self-destructive
habits, or by using the challenge to find our inner strength."*
−DALAI LAMA

I CAN'T FEEL MY HANDS AND FEET. MY BODY IS HEAD TO
toes pins and needles. It's one of the hottest days of the year
and I can't stop shivering. I'm regretting my decision to leave
work early.

*Why did I leave the safety of the gym? Where am I? It's too far
to go back now.*

The D is running slow. The subway platform has been smother-
ing me in humidity for twenty excruciating minutes. I crouch
down. I need to be closer to the ground. I cancel tonight's plans
with Lysia, going anywhere but home seems impossible. I send
her a text, "This is so bad."

The subway pulls up. It's too loud, the metal-on-metal ringing
through my ears. I question whether I should get on it. Some-

thing isn't right with me. The cool breeze of the air-conditioned car on my sweat-soaked body outweighs the prospect of climbing the stairs into the furnace of the city.

The subway is crowded. I find an opening between the doors and lean back. It feels good to take some weight off my legs. They're getting weaker by the second. My symptoms are getting worse. Cold sweat drips down my face and back. I'm hyperventilating. I don't know how I'm going to walk home when I make it to my stop.

I pick my head up long enough to make eye contact with a woman a few feet away. The look in her eyes scares the hell out of me. It's the look someone gives when they see something they shouldn't be seeing. Trying her best to hide what she's feeling, she musters a slight smile as she mouths the words, "Are you okay?"

I shake my head no and wake up staring at the subway floor, my temple pounding. Cries for help bounce around the subway car:

"Call 911!"

"Oh, my God, he's had a seizure!"

"Someone, get help!"

An MTA employee escorts me off the train at the next stop and places me on a bench. The EMTs arrive minutes later, asking me, "What's going on?"

"I don't know," I mumble.

I hold my hands up. They are frozen like lobster claws and I cannot open them.

"Your blood pressure is falling. It's going to be okay."

I vomit all over the platform. It's the most violent vomit I've ever experienced. The EMTs put me on a stretcher and take me for my first-ever ambulance ride.

Lysia meets me in the emergency room. I'm so thankful she's here. Incredibly, she's visiting from Seattle at the right time. It's incredible how she's been there at just the right time, more than once. I leave eight hours later, shaken but feeling the worst is behind me.

The ER has no idea what happened. I think it's food poisoning from the restaurant where I got lunch—vomiting, dehydration, a one-time thing. But a follow-up visit to the doctor revealed an abnormal EKG. "No big deal," he says. The follow-up echocardiogram comes back clean and he insists I have "nothing to worry about."

A reinforcement that this was an isolated event. I won't eat at that restaurant again. Problem solved.

A month later, a carbon copy of that day occurs again. Now the doctor is concerned with the abnormal EKG. I have an appointment with the head of cardiology at New York Presbyterian Hospital. I will undergo a stress test and wear a heart monitor for thirty days. The doctors don't want me experiencing another episode. They want to catch it in the act.

My legs are hollow, I'm weak, and my mind, hazy. I vomit periodically. My chest hurts. I believe any damage to my heart is my fault because I didn't accept it, I fought it's truth and I didn't listen to the warning signs. I put it in a box and ignored it.

To have come this far only to experience the threat of losing everything scares the hell out of me. I'm just starting to get this thing we call life. I have endured too much and come too far to be stopped now.

What I'm experiencing is a continuation of the secret to life, the gift I received from the universe, sitting at the picnic table in prison.

I wasn't aware I needed a reminder. Life thought differently.

Death and adversity are filters. The crap, the fears, anxieties, regrets, they don't make it through. What does make it through is the pure distillation of how I want to live my life. When the dross is removed, the mind is free; it's a beautiful feeling.

The crap, the fears, anxieties, and regrets require time and energy to process. They run in the background like an unused app on my phone, slowing other processes down. Allowed to run wild, they take processing power away from what is truly important.

My life since prison has evolved, the foundation has grown, the canvas expands every day. That gift was the foundation of what has become the filter through which I try my best to run my life.

I live life on my terms and in alignment with my vision and values. I pursue what I want because I enjoy the work, not for the outcome of perceived glory. Krishna told Arjuna he has the right to the labor, not the fruits of the labor.

The doctors never figured out what was wrong, and I accept that. I'm just grateful it hasn't happened again.

Sometimes our most painful experiences contain the very thing we need the most.

FIFTY-ONE

"Everything can be taken from a man but one thing: the last of the human freedoms—to choose one's attitude in any given set of circumstances, to choose one's own way."
—VIKTOR E. FRANKL

I HAVE AN UNEXPECTED DAY OFF, A BEAUTIFUL FALL Sunday. What to do with this gift of time? It's not a difficult choice. It's a gorgeous day and I'm taking advantage of it.

I take Metro-North out of the city and into Connecticut. I walk for hours on the sand, along the coastline, through hidden gardens. I take a break when I see an open bench with a killer view.

I'm reading *The Truth* by Neil Strauss. Two women are enjoying a walk. They ask if they can join me just for a second to remove rocks from their shoes.

"Of course," I say.

One of them catches a glimpse of the book cover, a neon pink heart with barbed wire wrapped around it.

"Ooh, that looks interesting. What is it about?"

They are my mom's age. For a moment I feel awkward explaining the book, then figure what the hell. We're all adults.

"It's the author's journey through depression, love, sex addiction, group sex parties, and swinging on his search for a meaningful relationship."

If the temperature of my cheeks is any indicator, they're as bright as the sun right about now.

"Oh! Well, that sounds interesting," one of them says. "Enjoy." They laugh and continue their walk, the other turning around to say, "You have the best seat in the whole park."

They're right, I do. The afternoon sun is reflecting on the water, the seagulls and egrets doing what they do. I love where I am right now. Being in nature's pure and beautiful presence.

I'd create a dramatic narrative if I say the government took my freedom; even better, they stole it. I'd draft a harrowing tale of conquering the evil oppressor, David vs. Goliath. People love these stories. They're fun; they make us feel good.

I can't tell that story. Nothing was stolen from me. I lost freedom because of the choices I made.

The effects were devastating. The glaring omission of something I didn't even know was mine to lose. The hole it left behind left no doubt about its existence. I found a gift within the devastation, one that I fight to never again take for granted.

Freedom is complex. It is deep. It goes beyond being confined to a perimeter. True freedom is found within, true freedom is internal, and the choices I make either contract or expand that freedom.

Every day there are hundreds of choices to be made. Some of them big, some of them small. Regardless of their size, bringing awareness to every choice is the key to an extraordinary life, to painting whatever I want to paint.

This blows me away. It makes me feel small and it makes me feel infinite. This is the power of choice.

The more effort I put into the canvas, the more choices I create. The more I choose to experience in life, the braver choices I make, the more opportunities and possibilities I create.

Jerzy Gregorek said, "Easy choices, hard life. Hard choices, easy life."

I used to think the opposite. I was wrong. I know what happens when I walk through the door. It's incredible. Every single time. Without fail.

My time, energy, and attention are all limited. They are nonrenewable. Once they are gone, they're gone forever. I have the power to choose how to utilize what can never be replenished.

Choices I took for granted now carry a meaning I will never again sacrifice.

How I spend my limited time and the actions I take.

I visit New York's incredible museums on rainy days. I go to Battery Park to gaze at the ferries going back and forth, with the Statue of Liberty as a backdrop. I daydream at the Classic Car Club of Manhattan.

Opening my closet and choosing what to wear. Walking to the kitchen, opening the refrigerator door, and choosing what to eat. Walking out my front door, choosing to go left or right. Sitting on the couch and choosing what to watch on Netflix.

Choosing to ask the girl I get lunch from every day on a date. Attending Toastmasters meetings every week and volunteering every week.

I'm learning there is no such thing as a small choice when the choice is made in awareness.

I've been asked if my crime was worth it. I've been asked if the money is buried in the backyard. A few people like to play the game. "Would you go back to prison for thirty days for a million dollars? Free and clear, no taxes. You'd be an instant millionaire."

My response: "I wouldn't do it for a billion. Not one day. There isn't enough money in the world."

The reactions are almost always the same: people get angry. They think I'm lying or maybe just stupid. "You're crazy," they say. "That's the stupidest thing I've ever heard. You don't know what you're talking about. Think about what you could do with the money."

I *have* thought about it. I don't think I'm stupid at all. I stand by my choice.

The moment I put a price tag on my freedom, I've already lost it. This, to me, is an extraordinary way to live.

FIFTY-TWO

"Now this is not the end. It is not even the beginning of the end. But it is, perhaps, the end of the beginning."
—WINSTON CHURCHILL

I KEEP THINKING I NEED AN END: A CLIMAX, THE ICING on the cake. I've realized this story has no end. Right now, there is only this moment.

I'm sitting in the sand at what may be my favorite place in the world. The tide is out, the beach stretching further than usual. Even though it's the end of October, I go swimming. Despite the 42-degree water temperature, I'm jumping in. I made a commitment to myself. I have to keep it.

I walk into the water to a point where it's deep enough to dive. Each step hurts. The freezing water hitting my head for the first time, even more so. Then it happens, a burst of pure energy and exhilaration. The pain was temporary and what was on the other side of it, extraordinary—something I need to remember.

Making and keeping commitments really works.

I dry myself as people look at me with confusion. The sun feels good, my dry clothes feel great. I reach for a book, *Live Your Truth* by Kamal Ravikant, starting where I left off.

I've read the book at least half a dozen times. I know it inside and out, and I don't know it at all. The same passages I've read multiple times now carry a new meaning. It's the kind of book that makes me stop and pause after each paragraph. I need to absorb what I just read. My world and, in turn, my life open a little more every time I read it.

Sitting in my beach chair, toes in the sand, this day is a gift. I'm learning they all are. But this day, low eighties, gentle breeze, sitting on a beach in New England in October. There's something special about this. I'm on the Long Island Sound. The waves are no higher than a foot tall. Even still, they are a symphony to my ears.

I'm exactly where I am meant to be at this moment. I'm at peace. Every lesson learned, every moment led me here.

This has been an incredible journey, the hardest of my life so far. I know there are still more obstacles. I know the past will catch up to me. I know I will once again lock myself in the prison cells of shame, not being enough, unworthiness, and fear. The difference is now I have the keys.

Right now, on this beach, at this moment, I am free. The canvas is no longer blank. I'm painting the life I want to live. I will make mistakes, the painting won't be perfect. I don't expect it to be. There are more doors to walk through. I know what I must do to live how I want to live.

What matters is this: each day, I paint a little more.

This moment is the end until the next one.

EPILOGUE

THIS JOURNEY STARTED ON OCTOBER 1, 2013, AND HASN'T stopped. The thing I'm learning by painting the canvas is that the journey to an extraordinary life doesn't end until we die. Clichés exist for a reason. It really is all about the journey.

There have been so many days I remember that I've shared with you. But there is one more, one that stands among the greatest nights of my life. I hate to hold one night up as mythical, perhaps growing grander with every recollection. Still, the truth is it was one of the most liberating and transformational nights of my life.

And finally, I have what I think is the best answer to the question I was asked.

THE EDDY, EAST VILLAGE NYC–JULY 27, 2016

We are the annoying table of adults who start talking the moment we sit down, the menu not even an afterthought. The restaurant fades into the background; our conversation drowns everyone and everything out. We are the only two people in the world—until our server walks over for the fourth time.

"No, sorry, we haven't even looked at the menu yet…"

This is only our second dinner together, yet there is a connection as though we've known each other across lives other than the ones we are currently living.

There is no small talk; we jump right in, pulling no punches. We hold nothing back. We are open, honest, and vulnerable. We share our darkest moments, then we laugh so hard, we cry. There is a unique bond between people who have seen the darkness.

This is the greatest emotional roller coaster ride I've ever been on, and I don't want it to end.

My mind is free from doubt, fear, and judgment. No ghosts of the past, no anxiety for the future. A pure, beautiful, powerful presence in this moment. I feel no pain as I speak of pain; nothing is holding me back. I've walked out of the cells I was locked in. Shame, guilt, embarrassment, fear, and ego are all gone.

I am free.

I'm in awe as she speaks, her beauty multiplying with every word. The more I learn, the more I want to know. I could talk to her all night into tomorrow. Her eyes, reinforcing the meaning of her name, radiate a light that exists only in the blackest of skies.

There is a question on the tip of her tongue, a desire to know more. She's seeking something. We all are. It's one of the things I love about her—her curiosity, her willingness to challenge the "shoulds" and expectations of a so-called normal life. She is carving her own way, and I'm fascinated by it.

I fall into her eyes as she searches for the right words. A spark and a delicious smile appear when she finds them. Leaning forward, she asks, "With all that you've experienced, how is it... how are you so happy?"

Wow. That's a big question.

I gave her an answer that night. I spoke about the foundational practices this experience has introduced me to and that I still practice today—meditation, journaling, and expressing gratitude. These have been instrumental in rebuilding my life, but there is much more than that.

The answer to her question is this book.

It's not an overstatement to say that this book helped save my life. Writing provided an outlet in a place where there were no other outlets. The process of creating this book was as cathartic as it was painful.

I remember the day I was sitting in the prison library when the pain reached a crescendo. I was annoyed that I was not in my usual spot. I was annoyed someone beat me to it. I had no idea how to write a book and what I was writing was causing me pain. I know how hard it is to have a book published. It seemed utterly pointless to continue. My mind whispers, *I'm in prison, living in my own hell. Why am I adding a level of torture to this experience?*

I flipped to an empty page and wrote, "Why am I doing this?"

The answer flowed without thought, without hesitation: *to help one person.*

I went back to what I was writing and the pain wasn't quite as bad.

When I was a kid, I loved to write. I forgot about this until Sean reminded me on his fateful visit, "You've always liked writing. Remember you wrote the script for Frank's driver's ed video? And you did the entire group English project for me—you, Rob, and Vinny—for Mr. Voss's class. I wish we still had a copy of that. And you wrote a draft for the high school play too."

It's funny the things we forget.

One of my happiest memories of childhood was straight out of a Norman Rockwell painting.

My friend Adam and I were fishing off a stone bridge, our short legs hanging over the water. We were using a stick with a piece of string and bread as bait. It's astounding how well this worked. Sometimes simple is more than enough.

I just started talking, telling a story that I was making up on the fly, with no idea where the plot was coming from and where it was going. It was the two of us and a crazy (for nine-year-old's) adventure on the golf course with a golf cart we found. I spoke for over an hour. Adam said it was the coolest story he had ever heard and told everyone about it.

I love creating and crafting ideas for books and movies. I was and am my happiest when I'm creative, when I put things together, when I connect the dots.

I didn't have to blow my life up to create the life I wanted. The opportunity was there, but I couldn't see it. Perhaps I had to, to learn what I have learned and to pass it on in the hopes it reaches someone who needs it.

Writing a book has been a secret dream of mine for as long as I can remember. As much as I love creating, the idea of a book was too big. I was too scared to start, to share, to be judged, to be criticized.

In order to protect myself, I kept the dream tucked away in the corner of my brain, content to live with the idea, not the finished product.

Well, now the product is finished, but the process is far from over. Writing is a two-part equation. The first half of the equation is reaching inside, dumping it on the page, being open, honest, and vulnerable.

The second half of the equation is where the magic happens. The second half of the equation requires that I face my new number-one fear: sharing.

Once I hit that button, the book is out there. It's no longer mine. If I don't complete the equation, I know the regret that waits for me. I'm guessing this book will sell twelve to fifteen copies. That doesn't matter. I must remember why I wrote this.

To help one person.

Not finishing, not hitting publish, not sharing, missing the opportunity to share my experience in the hopes of helping someone—that is a failure.

You reading these words means I walked through another door.

That is success.

ACKNOWLEDGMENTS

Thank you to my family and friends who helped make this book and dream a reality.

Mom, Aunt Bobbi, Dad, Paula, Sharon, Tim, Lynnea, Matthew, Sean, Christine, Emma, Qandeel, Elia, Ryan, Laura, Mason, Jill, Diana, Kamal, James, Dawn, Kim, Eric, Dharu, Amanda, Natalia, Terra, Osej, Dash, Dylan, Ken, Adele, Jana, Lysia, Jeff, Sal, Hassan, Ann, Don, Ioana, Nadia, and the Premier Toastmasters Club.

ABOUT THE AUTHOR

After hitting rock bottom, **CRAIG STANLAND** was forced to make a choice: give up or rebuild. He thought he had it all, until he lost sight of what is truly important and made the worst decision of his life, losing everything along the way, including his own self-worth. Through the painful, terrifying process of starting over, Craig ultimately discovered that when you have nothing, anything is possible.

Today, Craig is an author, speaker, and reinvention architect. He specializes in working with people whose lives have fallen apart, helping them reinvent themselves by showing them how to rebuild their self-worth and create the extraordinary lives they have always wanted. When he's not doing that, he'll most likely be found outside, at the beach, in the woods, or searching for vintage cars.

Find Craig online here:

Instagram: craig_stanland

craigstanland.com

Please feel free to email him at craig@craigstanland.com.

He would be honored if this book was reviewed and shared so that it may reach someone who needs it.

If you're in a dangerous place, please contact the National Suicide Prevention Lifeline: 1 (800) 273-8255.

If you're outside the US, please check suicide.org for a list of international hotlines.